World War Two

NEW FOREST

DISCOVERED

The areas Vital Contribution to the National War Effort

John Leete

Includes New Forest and Hampshire reference sections

'We must never forget the dedication and sacrifice of a generation and the human spirit that persists even against the most overwhelming odds'

Copyright © 2023 John Leete
First published in 2023

Based on the best selling title *The New Forest at War (Revised and Updated)*.

British Library Cataloguing in Publication Data

A catalogue record for this book is available from the British Library

Designed and typeset by Sabrestorm Publishing

Published by Sabrestorm Publishing, The Olive Branch, Caen Hill, Devizes, Wiltshire SN10 1RB United Kingdom.

Website: www.sabrestorm.com
Email: books@sabrestorm.com

ISBN 978-1-78122-023-8

Contents

Breamore House was used by the military and for a short time was HQ for General George S Patton (Breamore.com)

Foreword

Breamore House has been my family's home for ten generations. During WW2 it played it's full part in the war effort on the Home Front. Situated in the North-West of the New Forest, in Hampshire, bounded by Wiltshire and close to Dorset it's location was a considerable asset to the military.

Breamore House, as mentioned in the Reference Section of this title, was requisitioned in 1942. Initially, Breamore was occupied by the British Army and subsequently by the American Army. General George Patton stayed briefly in the house and used the Great Hall as his map room while planning the landings at Utah and Omaha beeches. He left quickly after his presence at Breamore was announced on German radio. There was a small landing strip in Butchers Field. Breamore was on the Avon stop line and was the base for a mounted division of the Home Guard.

We have always taken an interest in the contribution that the house and estate made and we are committed to ensuring that the dedication and sacrifice of The Greatest Generation is never forgotten. We hope that the history and events of what happened during WW2 will continue to be of interest and provide inspiration for future generations.

John Leete's book brings the history of the New Forest during the War to life with well researched material, a selection of fascinating photographs and personal anecdotes.

Michael Hulse
www.breamore.com

Preface

I started working for the New Forest National Park Authority in 2009 as an education and outreach officer on the Coastal Heritage Project, whilst finishing a Masters in Maritime Archaeology at Southampton University. Archaeology has always been a passion for me and something I have enjoyed and worked in since leaving school. The role as an education and outreach officer on an archaeological project was a new and engaging challenge that I was keen to put my mind to, as I wanted to share my passion and interest with others. The Heritage Lottery Funded Coastal Heritage Project was a great success, with a huge response to our education resources, talks, interpretation, website, and underwater film. This success helped secure further partnership funding for a new project: *New Forest Remembers – Untold Stories of World War II*, which I took on the challenge of managing. The Second World War is an especially important aspect of our heritage, and though there is a huge amount of historical interest and detailed specific independent research, little overall archaeological surveying had been carried out in the New Forest. As such, the area is a classic example of the paradox recognised by English Heritage that some of our most recent history and archaeology is fast becoming our rarest, as research focuses on older periods and evidence continues to be removed and forgotten. The New Forest Remembers project was a chance to reverse this trend, and to try to produce a more accurate record of what was happening in the New Forest during the Second World War, capture personal memories of the Forest and champion the work being undertaken by individuals and groups. The success of the information gathering that was undertaken has seen a tenfold jump in public archaeology records for the Second World War, but it is not just a recording exercise. Dealing with the war provides us with an opportunity to capture personal memories, photos, and documents, which can all be used to enhance the archaeological record. It is true that lots of information relating to the war still exists, but a lot of the material is in disparate archives, and work is required to link it all together and ensure long-term preservation. This is unique in an archaeological project: we have the potential to interview individuals who were based in the New Forest area and to add layers of additional detail to the sites we are studying. This provides us with a perfect opportunity to engage visitors, residents, and future generations with what might appear to be just a lump of concrete: a site that someone might pass off as rubbish can be understood for its important history and the human connection made, making it easier for visitors to relate to, and connect with it, and hopefully ensuring its future protection.

James Brown, Archaeologist
Former New Forest Remembers Project Manager.

For many people, the word archaeology instantly conjures up an image of Time Team digging trenches in sunny fields and discovering a plethora of fascinating artefacts. Yet behind any sort of archaeological investigation is a substantial amount of preparation and research. Nowadays, any sort of fieldwork is usually preceded by an archaeological Desk-Based Assessment (or DBA).

A DBA is conducted to assess the extent and potential of the archaeological resource in each area. Simply put, it is an opportunity to identify and review all the existing research material on a site, so that when any fieldwork is done the archaeologists and historians have the best possible idea of what to expect. A DBA may be done in advance of the building of a new housing estate, or even for the construction of something as small as a house extension. The DBA for the New Forest Remembers project was quite different; the overall study area was just over 1,000km². Fortunately, this massive study area was tempered somewhat by the smaller study period. A DBA is usually concerned with all periods of history, from the Stone Age through to the Cold War. I was therefore quite lucky that the study period for the New Forest Remembers project was so narrow (1935–47).

Nonetheless, the DBA would need to cover many hundreds of individual locations where Second World War activity took place, ranging in scale from the construction of an airfield to the digging of a slit trench. The research involved a wealth of sources, from Luftwaffe aerial photographs and period unit war diaries to modern LiDAR mapping and up-to-date national monuments lists.

A DBA of this size required a means of compiling all the data in one place. The most straightforward way of doing this was to construct a database into which information, sources and grid references of each identified site could be entered. The database could also be loaded into modern GIS mapping systems, allowing the sites to be visualised on a New Forest map. As each source of information became available, it was reviewed, and relevant information was entered into the database. The information derived from existing databases (predominantly the National Monuments Record, county Historic Environment Records, the Defence of Britain Database, and the National Mapping Project), contributions from local groups and societies (including the Beaulieu Estate and Friends of New Forest Airfields) and other sources, including archaeological reports and books, eventually identified 1,500 unique sites in the Forest. In many instances this did not even account for the many smaller elements of one site (such as the numerous individual buildings that make up one camp). Additionally, research into unit war diaries (a record kept by every unit active during the war) and historic maps identified some 600 other locations that were previously unrecorded or totally unknown.

Of these, some 120 sites were selected to be included in the DBA, therefore warranting extra attention from the New Forest Remembers team. These include sites that are well preserved, unique, or unusual facilities, and those that demonstrate the potential to provide more information from fieldwork.

The DBA was a thoroughly enjoyable text to write (all 54,000 words of it). As well as giving an extensive background to the overall role of the Forest during the war and the activities that took place, the history of each of the 120 sites was thoroughly researched and a full assessment of their importance and potential was produced. I am particularly pleased to have contributed in this way to the New Forest Remembers project.

Stephen Fisher, Historical Researcher.
Former Maritime Archaeology Trust.

Acknowledgements

I am indebted to the team at the New Forest National Park Authority upon whose original wartime memories project and mapping surveys this book is partially based. Without that support, and the kind contributions from and support of many other individuals and organisations, this title would not have been possible.

I extend my sincere thanks to everyone listed below. The list is alphabetical, rather than in any order of preference. If I have missed anyone, please accept my sincere apologies, and do let me know.

Chris Ashworth (The Family of)
Alison Barnes
Ian Bayley
Emma Blake
James Brown
Nick Catford
Sally Collier
Neville Cullingford
Mat Dickson
Mike Ellis
Dave Fagan, Hampshire Airfields
Stephen Fisher, Maritime Archaeology Trust
Simon Fletcher
Paul Francis
Guy Grasby
Frank Green
Liz Gregory (for the late Doug Gregory DFC)
Old English Inns
Hampshire Women's Institute (County HQ)

Laura Joyner
Kimberley Keay
Maxine Knott
Laura Lawton
John Levesley
William Lock
Ann Mattingly
Milford on Sea History Society.
New Milton Memorial Centre
New Forest and Hampshire WW2 Heritage
Gareth Owen
Hazel Robinson
Teresa Cammish
Lawrence Shaw
Tom Sykes, Coleshill Auxiliary Research Team (CART), especially for Chapter 9
Brian Taylor
Oliver Tobias
Andrew Walmsley
Will Ward
Richard Drew

With special thanks to New Forest Historian, Marc Heighway.

Abbreviations

Useful abbreviations mentioned throughout the book.

AA – Anti-Aircraft
ADS – Archaeological Data Service
AHBR – Archaeology & Historic Buildings Record
AMS – Air Ministry Standard
ARP – Air Raid Precaution
ATC – Air Training Corps
BCF – British Concrete Federation.
ENSA – Entertainments National Service Association – entertainment for Service personnel
FONFA – Friends of New Forest Airfields
GIS – Geographic Information System
GPS – Global Positioning System
GHQ Stop lines – Stoplines: Some tactical notes | The Pillbox Study Group Website. (pillbox-study-group.org.uk)
HCC – Hampshire County Council
HE – High Explosive
HER – Historic Environment Record
HLS – Higher Level Stewardship
HMS – His Majesty's Ship
LiDAR – Light Detection and Ranging
MoS – Ministry of Supply
MoW – Ministry of Works
NAAFI – Navy, Army, Air Force Institute (www.naafi.co.uk)
NFDC – New Forest District Council

NFNPA – New Forest National Park Authority
NFS – National Fire Service
NMP – National Mapping Programme
NRHE – National Record of the Historic Environment
NT – National Trust
PLUTO – Pipeline under The Ocean (taking fuel to the Normandy beaches)
PSP – Pierced Steel plank (American made temporary road/runway surface)
PX - The Army & Air Force Exchange Service (AAFES), also referred to as the Exchange and the PX or the BX
RASC – Royal Army Service Corps
RAF – Royal Air Force
RCAF – Royal Canadian Air Force
RSAAF – Royal South African Air Force
RCZA – Rapid Coastal Zone Assessment
RNAS – Royal Navy Air Service
SHAFE – Supreme Headquarters Allied Expeditionary Force
SMR – Scheduled Monument Record
SMT – Steel Mesh Track (temporary tracking used on some temporary airfields)
SOE – Special Operations Executive - Agents were mainly tasked with sabotage and subversion behind enemy lines (National Army Museum: www.nam.ac.uk)
STARFISH – Starfish sites were large scale night-time decoys used to simulate burning British cities. The purpose was to divert night bombers from their intended targets and to drop their ordnance over the countryside. Sites were created in the New Forest and close to main high-risk areas in Hampshire, such as the ports of Southampton and Portsmouth.
ST – Sommerfeld Tracking (temporary runway surface)
UKHO – United Kingdom Hydrographic Office
USAAF – United States Army Air Force
WI – Women's Institute
WLA – Women's Land Army
WVS – Women's Voluntary Service
WO – War Office

These are a few of the many abbreviations and acronyms but for those interested, many more can be found online via a search engine: Second World War Abbreviations and Acronyms - Researching WW2

Introduction

In remembering the legacy of the New Forest at war, we must first consider the people of the Forest, the area's history, and the climate on the road to war during the late 1930s.

The legacy is built upon these foundations, and this book helps to sets the scene through personal anecdotes, period news items and details of the state of the nation and aspects of wartime preparations. Whilst it is by no means an exhaustive account, it does however, provide a well-researched record, of the New Forest and its WW2 social and built legacy. The Forest, first recorded as a military training area in the sixteenth century, had a vital role to play in both world wars and more especially, during the preparations for and the launch of D-Day. Some Historians believe that the ultimate success of the campaign was in part because the Allied Armed Forces were able to harness so much power and might within the Forest ahead of 6 June 1944. This coastal location was recognised, as early as 1940, to be an ideal purpose-built springboard from which to launch a major component of the eventual offensive against Fortress Europe.

From 1937, men and women began to be mobilised for the emergency. Then during 1938 and 1939, factories were requisitioned for war production, Anderson air raid shelters were issued, and public shelters were erected. Gas masks by the million were distributed and Operation Pied Piper, the evacuation of children, pregnant women and the infirm culminated in late 1939. The whole nation was swept by tides of preparation, resolution, and by grim determination. At 11am on 3 September 1939 when Prime Minister Chamberlain announced '…this country is at war with Germany', preparations had already affected every citizen, every town, city and village, and every aspect of day-to-day life.

In the New Forest, as in other parts of the county of Hampshire, mobilisation was carried out with a mix of efficiency and confusion. Instructions, from the many and varied authorities going about their new wartime roles, changed almost daily. Local officials were left to interpret the instructions as they saw fit, and natural leaders, many with knowledge of the First World War, stepped forward and helped to make the best of the situation. However, because the coastline of Hampshire and the New Forest was close to mainland Europe, the authorities did not underestimate the need for a much more vigorous approach to preparation and defence in this area.

As people prepared themselves for life on the Home Front, so too the armed services and emergency services applied themselves to the mechanics of war. The New Forest had been used for military training for several centuries, and from 1939 and for the duration of the war, training continued in parallel with the expansion of the area's infrastructure and population. In 1935, the population was a little over 26,000, divided into three administrative areas of Lymington, Ringwood, and New Forest District. The population increased during the war years to a peak of approximately 70,000 in early 1944, comprising civilians, contractors, and services personnel.

After Dunkirk and the Battle of Britain, the early planning for a return to occupied Europe, later to be referred to as the 'Great Adventure' and by the military reference of D-Day, began to manifest itself at locations across the Forest. The Army, Royal Navy and Royal Air Force requisitioned country estates. By way of example, the Royal Air Force took over Beech House in Holmsley, and Breamore House near Fordingbridge became a base for British personnel, and later in the war, for American personnel. General George Patton was stationed at Breamore for a short time. The Pylewell Estate near Lymington was initially in use by the British Army, and it then served as a landing ground for the United States Army Air Force (USAAF). The Beaulieu Estate, the home of the Montagu family, became one vast military establishment. The training of agents of the Special Operations Executive (SOE) took place on the estate and naval craft and, later, sections of Mulberry were built on

Opposite page:
Top: *Runway construction, New Forest, 1942 (Authors Collection).* **Bottom left:** *A surviving shelter, New Forest, Hampshire (Marc Heighway).* **Bottom top right:** *The author with two members of the Exbury Veterans Association on D-Day plus 70 years (M.Knott).* **Bottom lower right:** *Part of SOE Agent display at the SOE Museum Beaulieu.*

A Piece of the parachute which dropped 'F' Section agent Yvonne Cormeau in France on the night of the 22nd/23rd August 1943. Her mission was to work as a wireless operator for George Starr's Wheelwright circuit in south-western France. She sent over four hundred near-perfect messages in difficult conditions, before being overrun by the successful Allied advance through France after D-Day.

the Beaulieu River. Various regiments and units were camped across the estate, and an airfield was built two miles away alongside the main road to Lymington, opposite what was the Beaulieu First World War airfield at Boldre.

Fawley All Saints Church displays flags of some of the WW2 Allied Nations

The Exbury Estate, which adjoins Beaulieu, became a Royal Navy shore establishment, known as HMS (also referred to in the Services as His Majesty's Stone Frigate) *Mastodon*, and legendary in many respects, not least for its association with the author and Technical Engineer Nevil Shute, and also, for being the site of the shooting down of a low-flying and over-crewed German aircraft, with the mystery surrounding that event, still unresolved to this day. In October 1940, the 1 regiment Compagnie de l'infanterie de l'air, Free French Forces, was based at Exbury and later, it was used by Free Polish Special Forces engaged in Operation Bardsea. This was the use of agents, drawn from Monika (Poland), deployed as paratroopers specialising in sabotage and subversive activities in specific operations just behind the bridgeheads on D-Day.

Great tracts of land across the Forest were used as training camps, tank driving schools, army camps, anti-aircraft gun sites, rifle ranges, mobile fire stations, stores, and ammunition depots. In parallel, airfields were constructed on many sites from Hurn (now Bournemouth International Airport) in the west to Beaulieu Heath in the east. Calshot air station, further east was already established as a flying boat base and during the war it served as an air sea rescue station.

Large houses were turned into hospitals, prisoner-of-war camps were erected, Air Raid Precautions (ARP) and fire service centres were created, and Local Defence Volunteers (LDV, later Home Guard) units were formed. The Forest was now the focus of much financial and practical input by civilian and armed services. Archive footage available at the Wessex Sound and Film Archive in Winchester shows some of the frantic activity that ensued. This included the building of new roads and the widening of existing routes, the felling of trees for the airfield construction programme, and later the creation of tented cities to accommodate the troops that moved into the area in the months before D-Day. At the peak of the construction programme records show that there were 20,000 builders and labourers employed across the Forest.

As the war progressed, there were recorded incidents of civilians being strafed by German aircraft, and bombs being dropped right across the Forest. Allied aircrews killed in action were being buried in Forest churchyards. Rationing was in force, although many local people were able to supplement their diets by living off the land. There was always the black market, and later in the war, when the Americans arrived, portions of fruit and meat plus sweets (candy) for the children, filtered out into local communities.

New friendships were forged, and by 1942 the Forest had become a cosmopolitan community. In addition to the Americans, there were service personnel from Canada, Pakistan, Ireland, India, Australia, New Zealand, Poland, South Africa, Czechoslovakia, and France (members of the Free French Army). Rumours were rife about the reasons for the sustained influx of men and machines, from 1943, especially as security was becoming noticeably tighter. Many people recalled how from early 1944, they were unable to visit certain parts of the Forest, and even those areas that it was possible to access, were very heavily policed. From each of the airfields, bombers and fighters flew many sorties in the days before 5 June (the original date for D-Day). Combat training intensified for the troops, and planning intensified too. There was time for recreation, but it was a nervous fun that these men experienced. The coastal waters were full of ships (records variously suggest between 4,000 and 7,000, but many smaller craft were attached to larger vessels and may not have been included in some of the counts). Great wartime leaders, including Churchill, Montgomery, and Eisenhower, visited many of the planning centres across the Forest, as did King George VI, who was said to have been particularly fascinated by the work being undertaken at Exbury.

With thousands of troops under canvas, twelve airfields with crews at the ready, many hundreds of vehicles, and thousands of tons of stores and equipment along the roads and under the trees, the Forest was soon to be at the forefront of a turning point in world history. As the invasion armada assembled in the Solent, along Southampton Water, the Beaulieu River and at other moorings, and embarkation began, no one could be in any doubt that the Allies were returning to Europe.

On the 6 June 1944, the Supreme Allied Commander General Eisenhower whose Operational Headquarters was at Southwick, near Fareham, Hampshire, gave the order to go. There was already a state of heightened readiness, and archive newsreel footage frequently used in historical documentary programmes, captured the scene at several of the local embarkation points.

Marion Loveland former WRNS on her 100th Birthday

Within days of the initial assault on Fortress Europe, the Forest was almost deserted. Fewer sorties were flown from the airfields, and the camps emptied as wave after wave of troops left to support the campaign in the days and months after 6 June. Some requisitioned properties were handed back to their owners, and the roads were empty of all, but a few military vehicles. Many commented on how eerily quiet the area was, however, day by day the Forest seemed to return to some sort of normality. Although the war in Europe, and the Far East, would last for another year, the people here were now as optimistic as they could be after so much turmoil and after so much time.

Today, the Forest is an established and popular visitor destination. In stark contrast to those turbulent days of 1939 to 1945, the Forest is tranquil, a place of recreation, relaxation, and leisure. This has only been made possible by the sacrifice of many and the determination of all. It is fitting that a selection of flags of some of the Allied Nations, on display at All Saints' Church, Fawley, is dedicated to the servicemen and women who were stationed in the New Forest. In this book, we remember those who gave their lives for the freedom of our generation, and for future generations. We can enjoy the Forest and its rich natural landscape, its wildlife, and its heritage thanks to visitors who passed through this area, decades ago.

This book chronicles aspects of the social, the military and the built history of the Forest, set against national and regional demands and operational climates. By no means is it likely that the story will ever be known or told in full, because every day another piece of the giant jigsaw of history is discovered.

The contents, with duplicated references to ensure continuity where necessary, have been compiled from many sources, including personal records, diary notes and interviews. Every reasonable effort has been made to ensure accuracy. I hope *WW2 New Forest Discovered* will permit readers to better understand our past, to treasure our heritage and to carry forward the history to ensure it is never forgotten.

John Leete,
Hampshire, England.

Marion Loveland was a WRNS Officer on duty on D-DAY
(Photograph Javaid Akhtar)

Marion Loveland

On 6th June 1944 I was an Officer of the Women's Royal Naval Service (WRNS), Assistant Secretary to the Commodore on duty at HMS Collingwood, a shore establishment in Fareham, Hampshire. The previous 24 hours had been relatively quiet however, none of us were in any doubt that something big was about to happen. There was a sense of excitement, mixed with anxiety and nervousness.

General Eisenhower was the Supreme Allied Commander for Operation Overlord, and he had his Headquarters a few miles away at Southwick House. He had been deliberating for hours before giving the order to the Invasion Fleet to GO! At Collingwood we were immediately at Action Stations and carried out our duties, communicating with the ships, in an urgent yet orderly manner. It was an extremely busy day to say the least and all around was a hive of tremendous and vital activity. The full impact of that day, which was to be a turning point in world history, was not obvious to most of us until sometime later, reinforced since then of course, by the annual commemorations and celebrations at home and in countries abroad.

I celebrate my birthday on 6 June and D-Day 1944 is one birthday I have never forgotten.

The camaraderie among personnel based at HMS Collingwood and the fact that we were all pulling together in a common cause, I am sure contributed towards our ability to do our jobs well and to successfully play our part in Operation Overlord. I believe it is particularly important to carry forward the story of WW2 to new generations. I am pleased therefore to be able to write these few words for John Leetes book about the vital contribution made by the New Forest and Hampshire and the massive undertaking by the men and women who served to achieve that. Everyone played their part.

Marion Loveland
WRNS HMS Collingwood 6 June 1944
Secretary (Retd.) of the Exbury Veterans Association (HMS Mastodon)
Hampshire, England

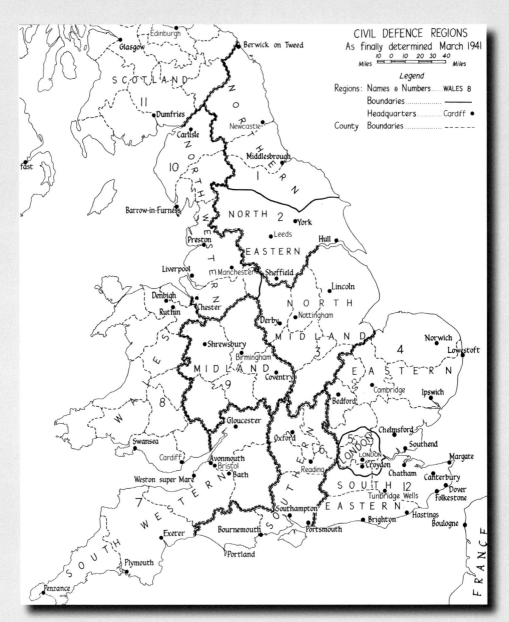

The New Forest was designated within AREA 6 Civil Defence Region HFRS

Preparations Against Invasion

The Government has had under consideration the question of the work which should be undertaken by Invasion Committees in the present phase of the war. The possibility of invasion of this country has not vanished and may again become imminent, but the immediate risk of invasion has for the present receded. The manpower problem is increasingly acute, and it is necessary to ensure that the time and energy of everyone in their county is directed in such a way as to secure the maximum contribution to the effort.

It has accordingly been decided that the work of Invasion Committees should be guided by the following principles.

1. It is essential that Invasion Committees, which form a vital part of the civilian organisation for the defence of this country against invasion, should continue in being, and should be maintained in a state of readiness to meet the risk of invasion should it again become imminent.

2. The preparation by Invasion Committees of civilian defence plans should be brought to a stage of completion appropriate to the circumstances of the area concerned within three months of the present date, but when this stage has been reached the plans should not be further elaborated unless and until the need should become more pressing, when further instructions would be given.

3. After the appropriate stage of completion has been reached it will be

necessary for the plans to be examined from time to time and kept up to date. The stage to which the plans of your committee should be brought within the next three months is set out in the Appendix to this letter. The Regional Commissioner appreciates that many Invasion Committees may already have advanced their preparations beyond this stage or may have problems peculiar to them which require to be settled even more urgently than those which area enumerated in the Appendix, but it is convenient to lay down a minimum standard which will be common to all.

The work of bringing the plans up to this stage should be confined to the members of the committee and to other executive officials' and organisations, such as the W.V.S. associated with it, so as to keep within the narrowest possible limits the diversion of the time of part-time workers who have other duties to perform.

Periodical meetings of the committee will be necessary to see that the plans of the committee are brought up to date and to keep members of the committee in contact. In addition, meetings of the committee should be held if ever circumstances require for instance if there is a change of Chairman or at the request of the military representative e.g., in the event of a modification of the military scheme of defence.

Invasion Committees will continue to participate from time to time in joint exercise with the military, but for the present these will be held at less frequent intervals and ordinarily over small areas. The reimbursable expenditure will be limited to what is required to meet essential stationery and telephone charges; etc. and such moderate expenditure as may be necessary on exercises. Publicity undertaken by Invasion Committees with a view to enlisting the interest and support or the general public in invasion preparations should be suspended for the present and no new approach to the general public, whether for information or otherwise, should be made.

The Regional Commissioner desires to emphasise that these instructions, which are issued by direction of the Minister of Home Security after consultation with the military authorities, do not involve any change in the role of Invasion Committees or in the high importance of the committees in the general scheme of the defence of this country against invasion. Their aim is to adapt the activities of committees to present circumstances while securing that the committees will be in complete readiness to fulfil the tasks which would fall to them in invasion. It is not proposed to make public announcement on the subject of these instructions, which should be regarded as strictly confidential to yourself and to the members of your committee. They may be communicated within the services for which members are responsible only to the extent necessary to enable them to be carried out. The Regional Commissioner would be glad if in communicating the instruction to the members of your committee you would explain their purpose and draw the attention of members to the importance not only of treating them in strict confidence but of avoiding in carrying them out, that creation of any impression that the government regards invasion precautions 45 are no longer necessary.

The Regional Commissioner wishes to take this opportunity of thanking as well personally the Chairman and members of the Invasion Committee, as all those who have been assisting them for their efforts in the organisation and planning of preparations against invasion during the past eighteen months. A great deal of devoted work has been put into this planning. The detailed and carefully compiled War Books will form a record of permanent interest. The Regional Commissioner believes that the team spirit, which has resulted from representatives of the various Services testing regularly to discuss the many problems of invasion, will be of lasting value.

Yours faithfully
N.E. PATERSON.
Principal Officer.
Hampshire.

To:
Chairman of Invasion Committees.

copies for information to: -
A.R.P. Controllers or Scheme Making Authorities.
Clerks of all Local Authorities.
Senior Regional Representatives of Government Departments.
Chief Constables (through R.B.S.O.)
Fire Force Commanders (through C.R.FO.)
Regional Administrator W.V.S.

APPENDIX

Chairman of Invasion Committees satisfy themselves that the plans which they have made have covered the following minimum requirement:

(i) Personal contact with the local representatives of all the authorities concerned with invasion preparations.

(ii) A review of the local military defence scheme in relation to civil premises and works of an immovable nature (e.g., hospitals, reservoirs, etc) to ensure that wherever possible the protection of these is included in the scheme.

(iii)The making of arrangements for civil collaboration with the military in operations, e.g., the choice of a centre of communications between the military and civil authorities and the devising of an operational procedure for contact between the local Military Commander and the Invasion Committee.

(iv) A preliminary review to discover the size of the local problem involved in the following:

Messenger Service.
Unofficial First-Aid Arrangements.
Emergency cooking facilities.
Emergency drinking water supplies.
Additional Rest Centre accommodation for the homeless.
Compilation of registers of labour, tools, and transport.

A note should be made of the chief difficulties and the main points on which effort would have to be concentrated if it became necessary to provide the above facilities, and responsibility should be allocated for the preparation of detailed plans at short notice.

(v) Ensure that all the above plans and relevant particulars are recorded in the War Book.

The popularity of dance bands extended to many military bases
(AVM Photo)

1

Music while you work

In the immediate pre-war years of the 1930s, Britain was undergoing changes, socially as well as in its industrial and technological capabilities. The country was slowly, but finally throwing off the legacy of the First World War, yet it was still trying to cope with the aftermath of the Depression (also known as the Great Slump).

Fortunately, the high unemployment levels began to decrease during 1934, and two years later they decreased further when the government simultaneously embarked on two major projects, road building and ship building, to stimulate growth. The inter-war years programme for building airfields (known variously as the expansion programme and the emergency planning project) also created work from the mid-1930s. Underpinning the social changes, was the availability of news, not just through the newspapers, but crucially via the radio (or the wireless as it was known), which was widely accessible throughout the country, mainly thanks to the BBC. Whilst in many ways the radio service was still in its infancy, it quickly became an integral part of the day-to-day lives of most folk. By the outbreak of war, and for the duration of WW2, the radio played a vital role in keeping the mind, soul, and spirit of the nation together by broadcasting music, motivating speeches from Churchill and a mix of light entertainment. It was also a powerful propaganda weapon and was used to great effect to deliver censored news programmes.

The newly built Broadcasting House stood impressively against the skyline on that wet December morning in 1932. Its moderne curves, cast in Portland stone were complemented with floor to ceiling windows on the ground floor and the array of exterior sculptures. Inside, the new paint and polished wood of the corridors were comparable to a 1930s luxury ocean liner, and every detail from the lights to the door handles had been carefully considered to ensure that the building was as cutting edge as the technology it was designed to accommodate. In Studio 3B on the third floor, an historic event was about to take place. J.H. Whitley, Chairman of the Board of Governors of the BBC, stood in front of the microphone as the red 'on air' light blinked twice and then stayed on. With that, the very first words of the new Empire Service were on the air, beamed from a wintry London to the sunshine of Australia and New Zealand. The power to bring together voices from countries across the world, was also a vital and tangible link across the British Empire. It was demonstrated on Christmas Day 1932, in a message spoken by King George V and broadcast from a temporary studio created at Sandringham House, Norfolk. The words, written by Rudyard Kipling, referred to the 'unifying force' of technology, and began as follows:

Through one of the marvels of modern science, I am enabled this Christmas Day to speak to all my peoples throughout the Empire. I take it as a good omen that wireless should have reached its present perfection at a time when the Empire has been linked in closer union, for it offers us immense possibilities to make that union closer still. It may be that our future will lay upon us more than one stern test. Our past will have taught us how to meet it unshaken. I speak to you now from my home and from my heart to you all, to men and women so cut off by the snows, the desert, or the sea that only voices out of the air can reach them.

As the sound of a global family sharing common interests, the broadcast made a huge impact on its Empire audience of twenty million. Yet few could have realised at the time that the Empire family would be drawn even closer by war, just a few years hence.

In Germany in 1932 the Nazi Party came to power, and at the beginning of the following year Adolf Hitler became German Chancellor. In America in 1932 President Roosevelt was elected to the first of his three terms of office in the White House, and on 1 January 1933 Japan attacked China in breach of a League of Nations agreement. The British Empire had interests in all these countries, and yet there seemed to be little appetite for, or concern expressed about, worldly issues. This was the era of Al Capone, the Loch Ness monster, the game Monopoly, Amelia Earhart, the era when air conditioning was invented and the Hindenburg airship crashed, when the helicopter was invented, and the first demonstration of radar was given. This was when Rowntree created the Kit Kat and when Chamberlain announced that there would be, 'Peace in our Time'. This was the 1930s, a decade that was riddled with contrast and paradox, the decade when the words 'streamlined' and 'glamorous' became fashionable and acceptable additions to the English language, and a decade when the English language itself was, now thanks to the wireless, entering a new era of mass communication.

The cinema provided entertainment as well as keeping people informed. Mobile cinemas travelled the country, setting up in halls and works canteens

Doreen Price remembers Radio Normandie, which broadcast into the south of England:

We saw a poster in a shop window in Bournemouth, which was advertising Radio Normandie and its programmes. They were sponsored in those days. I know Victor Silvester was on one of the programmes because my mother loved his music. I know the children's programme was presented by someone called Uncle Chris. When the war came, the station stopped broadcasting.

Radio Normandie was on the air from 1926 to 1939. Programmes went out primarily on records, which were made in London however, some programmes were broadcast live. It was not just verbal communication that was increasing as the wireless started to reach the masses; visual communication in the form of films and newsreels was also entering a new phase. Films were shown at huge luxury cinemas such as the Rex, the Rialto, the Odeon, and the Roxy, which were being built at the rate of three per week across the country. Cinemas were always full; anyone with style would want to be seen taking tea in a cinema restaurant, dolled up to the nines. Going to the cinema became part of a culture of 'escapism'. This encompassed a new freedom of expression, something that the public had not experienced before or during the First War, or through the Depression-hit years of the 1920s.

This freedom was everywhere, including in music, where the new era of big swing bands, crooners and dances had begun. The mood seemed to be: 'Let us welcome the American take on life for today we are young and tomorrow, well, who knows what tomorrow will bring.'

In sedate Britain there were, perhaps inevitably, letters to the papers about the dangers of too much liberation for the masses, the evil that, for example, 'dance' brought with it, even suggestions that modern dance was the devil's dance. Ironically the Establishment seemed to resent change and popular culture because it was the establishment, that controlled almost every aspect of life, including, radio technology.

Betty Hockey was a member of a concert party that toured military bases across Hampshire (Betty Hockey)

On the BBC a not untypical National Programme was that of Saturday 21 August 1937. Henry Hall's Dance Orchestra was on the wireless at 12.30pm, followed by cricket reports. Later there was organ music and forty minutes of accompanied singing. There were short stories, orchestral music, talks on chastity, humility and obedience, news and weather, and a show featuring the singer, Jessie Matthews. This was called 'Past, Present and Future', and how apt that was, at a time when the country was now making preparations, for war.

Demand existed, however, for more popular music, especially for dance band music and hot jazz. To exploit this, a private company, the International Broadcasting Company (IBC), was set up. It hired airtime from overseas stations and transmitted popular programmes aimed at the British market from Radio Lyon, Radio Normandie, Radio Athlone, Radio Méditerranée and Radio Luxembourg. By 1938, Radio Luxembourg had 45 per cent of the Sunday listening audience against the BBC's 35 per cent. When war broke out, commercial broadcasting into Britain ceased, not least because Radio Luxembourg's transmitters fell into Nazi hands. Yet it was stations such as Luxembourg that first brought swing and big bands, and famous American names, to the British wireless listener; and their popularity grew.

Now without commercial radio from Europe, more gentle music was still being played by the traditional dance bands of Jack Hylton, Percival Mackey, Ambrose, and a whole host of others. Gradually, however, there was a marked shift towards the more popular swing, although this was, initially anyway, less strident than the sounds that had been coming from the American bands, sounds that audiences in Britain would eventually be able to hear live when some of those bands played in theatres and open-air concerts on the nations Home Front.

Bill Percy, who was stationed near Brockenhurst, said:
I remember when we were sent for special training in London, we spent our 24-hour pass to see the Savoy Orpheans. A live band was a great new experience for us, and I enjoyed that type of music right up until I lost my hearing. We did have several live concerts performed by an ENSA troop while we were under canvas.

The BBC however, regained its monopoly, and throughout the war years delivered, in accordance with the government's instructions, programmes such as '*Music While You Work*', which was broadcast over war factory loudspeaker systems and intended to boost morale and to keep industry running. '*Workers Playtime*' was a live broadcast more often than not, from 'A factory canteen somewhere in Britain'.

The wireless was to make a major contribution to the lives of men, women and children, and members of Britain's armed services at home and overseas, throughout the Second World War. Its positive impact was measured quite unscientifically by a doctor who transferred to Lymington Hospital in early 1944: 'People talk quite incessantly about wireless programmes and how they enjoy the escapism it gives them. They talk of band leaders and singers, comedy stars and stories as though they are personally involved with each. For some it seems a better tonic than I can prescribe. Thank goodness'. It was indeed the mix of music, songs, and short stories, as well as gardening and household tips, children's programmes and sports reports that helped everyone carry on regardless.

And so it was Christmas
Photograph: Authors Collection

2

Christmas 1939

'Please Mr God, take me home to my Mummy. I hate it here.' This is an extract from a note written by nine-year-old evacuee Sidney Wallace who, with two other younger children, had been 'fostered' by a middle-aged couple living near Ringwood. Evacuated from the Midlands on 31 August 1939, Sidney was about to spend his very first Christmas away from home, away from his mother, Daphne, and his older sister, Betty, who had enlisted with the Red Cross. He was also separated from his younger sisters, Marion, and Pauline, who had also been evacuated, but who were in Wiltshire. William, his father, had joined the Navy in 1937 and had been posted overseas. Sidney knew that Christmas was not going to be the same as the wonderful ones he had enjoyed before. As much as he loved adventures, this was one he wanted to escape from. It was not anything like what he had expected or previously experienced. He was now getting up at five o'clock every morning, helping his 'foster parents' with the other children, helping with the housework, including 'dirty' jobs such as cleaning the toilet and the scullery floor. There was little time for exploring the surrounding area or even playing with his fellow evacuees. Sidney was nothing more than an unpaid servant. This was very unfair, and he needed his mum more than anything. He had more questions than answers. Was this going to be the worst Christmas he had known in his young life? It felt odd, as though he was having a bad dream. Soon he hoped he would wake up, see his mum, then run towards her as fast as his little legs could manage, so she could give him the biggest cuddle ever. Sidney though was later moved to a new home near Brockenhurst where life improved and he felt safe and happy.

Another aspect of evacuation troubled a local diarist that December 1939. He pointed out that most people were 'doing their share' by accepting evacuees willingly, but there were still many big houses in the Forest that remained half empty. Wanting to stop what he saw as selfishness and waste, he also expressed concern that there were still people squandering huge sums on luxurious living while many others were unable to provide even minimal shelter and clothing for themselves. Yet those with money could, if they wished, spend it on helping the war effort.

The local branches of the Salvation Army were amongst those calling for additional funds at Christmas, in their case to purchase mobile canteens at a cost of £250 each and to set up rest clubs for £1,250 each. Across the Forest, as the numbers of service personnel grew during the war years, the weight of demand upon the 'Sally Army' became heavier, not least upon the volunteers, yet they were there and always ready to serve.

Twenty-five-year-old Tom Clarke had joined the Grenadier Guards and spent his first Christmas on exercise in the New Forest. Common among his comrades, almost all of whom were new recruits and many of them younger than him, there was a feeling of resignation that Christmas 1939 was going to be a turning point. They knew from their fathers and grandfathers who had served in the First World War that 'Hope is good, but reality is what you get, and nothing is ever the same again.' As much as they hoped the war would be over soon, they were facing up to the fact that there would be much death and destruction, and if they and their families survived, the world would be a vastly different place to the one they knew. So, although Christmas was a welcome break, it was unlikely to distract them from what lay ahead.

In the Solent and along the south coast of England, Trinity House vessels lay at anchor, helping to guide ships home for Christmas. Several of the lights had been mechanised, but for the crews on the other Trinity House vessels it was a precarious balance between keeping themselves safe from enemy attack, coping with the isolation and trying to enjoy a Christmas at sea away from their loved ones. The lightship men were regarded by the popular press as symbols of a burning hope, and beacons of an undarkened faith. 'In carrying on their lonely task, they are preserving for the rest of us, the very spirit of the Christmas season,' wrote one journalist.

Another journalist, meanwhile, had visited Lyndhurst, where a woman complained that since everyone was fighting for their very existence, there was no justification

Newspapers carried advice on how to make the best of Christmas despite the shortages

for a Christmas break for munitions workers. No one denied that production during every hour of every day was of vital importance, but her concern was that workers desiring holidays were showing a fundamental inability to grasp the gravity of the situation!

In his Christmas sermon, the Archbishop of York was to reflect the mood of the nation well, certainly its desire for guidance, reassurance, and hope. Listeners across the New Forest huddled around their wirelesses. The words of the sermon resonated with their own feelings; Christmas, usually a time of joy, was now a time of disbelief and anxiety. The archbishop spoke about the dangers of escaping from reality, the need for moral revolution and what could be done to comfort each other. This sermon, many noted, was 'Churchillian' in nature: inspiring yet realistic; a morale-boosting effort that went some way towards encouraging everyone to be positive.

Among the many rumours that the population had to contend with in the days leading up to the first wartime Christmas was the belief that married women and widows would be asked to surrender their wedding rings to help the government pay for the war. The rumour circulated again a year later, most likely prompted by the fact that in Italy under Mussolini women were indeed required to give up jewellery and rings.

As depleted families around the country sat down at the table, as those evacuees and the hundreds of orphaned children from Europe spent their first Christmas with strangers, and as the men and women who had been called up for duty in civilian roles and for service in the Forces lined up in the canteens, sat in makeshift shelters or joined their hosts, the spirit and meaning of the season brought them together.

For at least on that one day, the nation felt united. As a diarist recorded for a radio programme that was broadcast after the war, 'We knew then that whatever was to come, we would give of our best, we would strive to win through, and we would overcome the challenges for the sake of our children and the survival of our country and the free world.'

King George VI was not a competent speaker, yet through his Christmas broadcast he succeeded in galvanising his people, He ended his speech with a quote from a poem written in 1908 by Minnie Louise Haskins:

I said to the man who stood at the Gate of the Year,
Give me a light that I may tread safely into the unknown.
And he replied:
"Go out into the darkness and put your hand into the Hand of God.
That shall be better than light, and safer than a known way."

In stark contrast to this, across the North Sea the population of Germany had by Christmas 1939 already been subjected to six years of propaganda, which had led them to believe that the country was mighty and just, in bringing war to Europe. The message was all about uniting German people in a righteous cause; yet when blackouts, rationing and winter relief campaigns became compulsory, privately and in hushed circles many started questioning the cause they were supporting. At Christmas, there was *Eintopf,* which was described by American correspondent William Shirer thus: '*Eintopf,* a one-pot meal which means all you can get for lunch is a cheap stew. But you pay the price of a big meal for it, the difference going to the winter relief, or so they say. Actually, it goes into the war chest.'

German girls had already had a taste of things to come through membership of the Bund Deutscher Madel (BDM), the League of German Maidens. They reported for duty on the Home Front, and by that first Christmas of the war their indoctrination was well under way. They lost their individuality in order to become wholly hardened, their simple identical dress and enforced lack of makeup helping to further the eradication of personal thought and deed. The Hitler Youth movement was helping to spread anti-Semitism and was also recruiting new members to the armed services, especially the SS. The Schutzstaffel, or Protective Echelon, the black-uniformed elite corps of the Nazi Party, had been founded by Adolf Hitler in April 1925 as a small personal bodyguard, but had grown with the success of the Nazi movement and, gathering immense police and military powers, had become virtually a state within a state. Over half a million people, mostly the young, the sick and the infirm, had been evacuated into the countryside, and they would spend that first Christmas away from their loved ones. Swastika flags were everywhere, and many homes used them instead of traditional decorations. Set against the bleakness of life for the majority, and the controlled society, the Nazi machine was working flat out even on Christmas Eve just to reinforce its message and the expectations it had of its people. Berlin's *Morgenpost* (Morning Post) ran an article headlined 'Rudolf Hess addresses an unmarried mother':

As all National Socialists know, the highest law in war as in peace is as follows, preservation of the Race. Every custom, law and opinion have to give way and adapt itself to this highest law. Such an unmarried mother may have a hard path, but she knows that when we are at war it is better to have a child under the most difficult conditions than not to have one at all. It is taken for granted today that a woman and mother who are widowed or divorced may marry again. It must also be taken for granted that a woman who has a war child may enter marriage with a man who is not the father of that child. A race, especially during war, cannot afford to neglect to keep and continue its national heritage. The highest duty a woman can perform is to bear racially healthy children. Be happy good woman that you have been permitted to perform this highest duty for Germany.

Around the New Forest as elsewhere in Britain, people tucked into the first wartime Christmas dinner. Jess Walker of Holbury recalled toasting absent friends, a swift end to the war and a better tomorrow:

Many of us were trying out new recipes using provisions very carefully in case of shortages, and we had to add a great deal of imagination. It was for our generation a strange almost unreal contrast between celebrating Christmas and knowing that we were at war again, and that the suffering was just beginning. We went out for a walk later in the day and stood for a while taking in the Forest landscape and we wondered if all this would be lost. Fortunately, it was to be lost to our own army for the duration of the war rather than to an occupying enemy, so there was hope in life.

And so, it was Christmas, despite everything.

Watching and waiting for the nightly raids outside the family shelter. (Photograph: Wayne Johnson)

3

The War
had come to us

Having thus far set the scene and reflected on the state of the nation and the world, and the initial effects of war on the New Forest and its impact on local communities, we have the foundations upon which to build the next phase of the story.

Specifically, whilst we form an idea about how the war was to physically affect the Forest and its people, we can also begin to understand the extent of the social changes. It is the social changes which have left us with a tangible legacy of those far off and desperate days; days that will soon no longer be within living memory. Whilst remains of the built environment are evidence of the core role of the area during its occupation by Allied armed services during the war years, it is vital that we continue to record and document the, all too easily lost, social legacy. Every snippet of information and every faded photograph, every anecdote and every memory will have a place in history when those, for whom the war was a personal experience, pass, and when our ability to touch our heritage will be immeasurably diminished. We will be even more reliant upon written testimony, testimony that tells us of the reality of lives lived: the rationing, blackouts, make do and mend, war funds weeks, evacuees, queuing, knitting for the troops, rules and regulations including compulsory carrying of gas masks, recycling, and tending to allotments. Many records speak of helping each other, camaraderie, walking miles to visit family and friends, visits to the cinema, comforting the bereaved and missing brothers, husbands, fathers, and lovers.

Anecdotes about the initial influx of evacuees in 1939 overwhelming the Women's Institute (WI) at Milford on Sea contrast with stories of 'strange goings on' in Sway, which were eventually revealed as being night training exercises by the Local Defence Volunteers (LDV) later the Home Guard. They speak as well of one of the air raids on New Milton, which killed nineteen civilians and several servicemen. Jim Gould vividly remembers the horror of seeing a car on fire at the crossroads in the centre of the town, with the occupant being consumed by the flames. The fierce fire prevented any attempts at rescuing the driver. Jim was 'frozen on the spot, stunned at what I was seeing'. Another witness, Jude James, says that there was a controlled panic:

The war had come to us and although we had been preparing for it, the suddenness and ferocity of the attack against the town caused some people to run, others simply to rush forward to see what, if anything they could do to help. There was a lot of screaming. As a youngster that upset me a great deal.

Official documents prepared ahead of the war by the Emergency Planning Committee included planning for incidents like this: 'It was reported that there were 7800 spaces available in cemeteries throughout the district. Subject to certain agreed rules and regulations, ten churches in the area were prepared to permit the use of their buildings as temporary mortuaries.'

There are also anecdotal records telling of enemy aircraft strafing New Milton's railway line, the station, and the bridge in Station Road. Young children, who had been trainspotting, scrambling for cover. On a lighter note, just a few steps north of that railway bridge was Dorothy's Café, which opened in 1940 and, as personal anecdotes reveal, very quickly became a meeting place for locals, airmen from Lymington and Holmsley airfields and many service personnel who were passing through the town. Noted for both its home-cooked food and its home-from-home atmosphere, it remained in the ownership of the same family until about 2016 when the building was sold for redevelopment. It was for many years, a tangible social legacy of the wartime era where one could engage older local customers in conversations about the area's wartime history.

The Memorial Hall in Whitefield Road is the successor to a building that was erected on the site in 1930. The land was purchased by the post-First World War Brother-

Dorothys Cafe opened on this site in 1940 (Authors Collection)

hood from Milton Unionist Club (Conservative Club) by a conveyance dated 31 December 1929. The Public Hall, as it was then known, must have run into difficulties during the Second World War because eventually, in February 1943, it was let to the local firm *Moody Son & Co.* as a furniture repository. With the coming of peace in May 1945, the people of New Milton cast about for a suitable memorial to all the men and women from that part of Hampshire who had lost their lives, and the *Lymington Times* dated 1 September 1945, published the first list of donations for the purchase of the hall as that memorial. It was to be used as the British Legion local headquarters and as a community centre for the town. The Trust deed said that if the Legion could not continue the successful management of the Hall, it was to call a public meeting for residents to decide its future. And so, in 1945, the War Memorial Hall started its new life, and it remains today as a symbol of remembrance.

Records tell of schools that were evacuated to safe areas. For example, Portsmouth Grammar School in Hampshire relocated to Brockenhurst School. Vera Wallis of Ringwood remembered: 'Where evacuees increased local school populations, classes were often taken on a half-day basis. Half-a-day's schooling for local children in the morning, with evacuees being taught in the afternoon, for example.'

Local people who opened their homes to the evacuees were paid the sum of 10s 6d (52 pence) per week, although this was reduced to 8s 6d (42 pence) per child if two or more children were billeted at the same address.

In some areas, teachers from evacuated towns and cities were drafted in to help with the additional workload placed on small country schools. For evacuees, it was reassuring to have someone from their own community, for example their own teacher, with them.

People walked or cycled everywhere, but even their personal mobility was affected fundamentally by the war because security became and remained a primary concern.

Lord (John) Teynham, recalled that, *As a child I was stopped at the gated entrance to the cottage where I had been rehoused, near the airfield built on the family's estate. A huge giant of an American GI checked my ID card every time I left and returned to the cottage.* In addition, privately owned vehicles were taken off the road because the owners were not entitled to petrol coupons. However, a number of cars, lorries and vans were requisitioned by various government departments, local authorities, and the emergency services, so they could fulfil the vastly increased duties of those organisations. There were exemptions, including vehicles used by doctors and members of the Women's Voluntary Service. Petrol was available for farmers and those engaged in other vital work for the war effort. Betty Hockey, who ran the Non-Stops Concert Party, which toured various military camps around the Forest, was able to secure enough fuel to meet all their performance commitments:

It was considered we were keeping up the morale of the servicemen and women and so we never really had problems about getting fuel. Later in the war when the Americans arrived, they gave us all the fuel we needed. Well after all, we were entertaining a lot of GIs* by then.

Car sharing was both popular and necessary, as was hitch-hiking, which according to some records, peaked in 1943 and again in 1945. To get around the problem of petrol rationing, people came up with alternative methods of power, including gas which was stored on the roof of vehicles in large, sealed bags. The bicycle became the main form of transport, although walking was for many the only and obvious way of getting to and from their destination. Later in the war, the road system across the Forest became the subject of attention. According to the records of the Forest's Verderers' Court: 'Ahead of D-Day nearly 25 miles of road were widened an average of 4 feet, and this effectively removed from general use, 25 acres of Forest land.'

Train travel was severely restricted during the war years, with Armed Services personnel being given priority. During the build-up to D-Day in 1944, further restrictions were placed on the railways. Posters were used as part of a massive propaganda campaign to ask, 'Is your journey really necessary', and to encourage passengers to 'give your place to a member of the fighting services'. Lilian Maxwell, formerly of

---

*GI means General Issue and was stamped on US equipment. It was the nickname given to American soldiers.

The site of a former Heavy Anti-Aircraft Battery site at Yew Tree Heath Brockenhurst (March Heighway)

Bransgore, remembered that these posters were just a few of thousands that were displayed, covering subjects such as gardening, the enemy, collecting money and scrap for ships and aircraft, knitting for the troops, health and make do and mend:

You must remember that the wartime generation was very susceptible to such campaigns, and we never questioned the messages and instructions that we were given. Even adverts in newspapers and magazines for items such as toothpaste and shoe polish had either a slogan or an image that linked them to the war effort.

Cinemas and the wireless were also pivotal in the success of the propaganda campaign, and there was a whole genre of wartime films, some made in America, that were scripted and filmed in such a way as to boost the morale and lift the spirit of the people. *Mrs Miniver, Went the Day Well? Tawny Pipit* and *A Canterbury Tale* were among some of the greatest of all patriotic flag-waving films, which were screened in cinemas such as the Regal in Ringwood, (subject to possible resurrection as a cinema, although it is presently derelict), the Waverley in New Milton (long gone), the Lyric in Lymington (now a shop) and the Regent in Christchurch, now an arts centre and cinema. These and other local cinemas, most since demolished, welcomed Americans from local Forest airfields and service personnel from many Allied countries. In addition to these memories and anecdotes, remains of the wartime built environment, such as pillboxes and pieces of concrete runway, hard-standings and so-called temporary brick buildings, will, through the efforts of the New Forest National Park Authority and the myriad of historical and preservation groups in the area, for many years to come, hopefully, continue to provoke thoughts about and promote consideration of the many thousands of men, women and children for whom the Forest was home during the Second World War. Original diary notes and letters are also excellent sources of information from which we can continue to learn much about the people and the places, as in this example from a wartime diary: 'Eling Tide Mill, near Totton, supplied water to the nearby Fawley refinery, which in turn supplied fuel via the Pipeline under the Ocean (PLUTO) to the shores of France. Eight Marines were assigned the task of guarding Eling, although they all complained that they wanted to see more action than Eling could ever provide.'

Memories of wartime are also inspired by the memorials that have been erected by local organisations and authorities across the Forest to commemorate the personnel who served. Standing by one such memorial set some 50ft above a beach, watching the waves gently folding back on themselves as they hit the pebbled shore, it is extremely hard to imagine that today's calm scene reflects in any way, the reality of those desperate days when men and machines were prepared for what was referred to by some commentators as 'The Great Adventure'. We are at a place called Lepe (pronounced leap), or more specifically Lepe Country Park, which for many visitors to the area will be the first window on the wartime history of the New Forest. Lepe is at the southern end of Southampton Water, overlooking the Isle of Wight, with Bournemouth Bay to the west and Portsmouth to the east. If anyone wants to know where this hamlet is, most of those offering directions will probably say 'It's near Beaulieu.' Well, yes, it is, and it is not far from Exbury House and Gardens either.

Here you can discover the story of PLUTO. Operation Pluto was a joint operation between British engineers, oil companies and armed forces to construct oil pipe-lines under the English Channel between England and France in support of Operation Overlord. The scheme was developed by Arthur Hartley, chief engineer with the Anglo-Iranian Oil Company. You can also find out about the Mulberry Harbour, the Women's Royal Naval Service (WRENs), which operated small craft, even on stormy winter days, and Operation Neptune, which was the cross-Channel phase of Operation Overlord. Operation Neptune placed all naval issues under the command of Admiral Bertram Ramsey, whose command skill had already been seen in 1940 when he played a vital part in the evacuation of troops from Dunkirk. During the build-up to D-Day, columns of Sherman tanks were parked under the pine trees here. The Sowley boom anti-submarine net was strung out under the sea from a position close to the beach. It was only recently removed when it was deemed a hazard to shipping. For such a small area Lepe made such a huge contribution to the war effort; it is just overflowing with history. When you visit, you can enjoy the especially useful audio tours, or if you prefer, explore, take photographs, then go away and read the reference books. Perhaps you will be able to find someone who

Top: *A fine example of a surviving pillbox at Milford on Sea (Marc Heighway)*
Bottom: *Remains of Dragons Teeth Defences and beach defences at Taddiford Gap near Milford on Sea (Marc Heighway)*

can talk first-hand about the place, for there are still those who, like Tom Charlton, were youngsters during the war:

We were not evacuated during the war because we lived in a so-called safe area in the Forest and we could get on our bikes and ride around although when it got to spring of 1944, things started to change, and a lot of roads were closed, and areas shut off to the public. We came down to Lepe a few times and it was exciting seeing all the activity. We thought it was just another military camp and it was not until after D-Day was it clear how important it was. After the war we came and played on the site and there was still a lot of concrete and a lot of discarded material.

From several hundred feet in the air, footprints of buildings and concrete emplacements, including the remains of Mulberry construction, can still be seen quite clearly. This area, integral to the massive build-up for D-Day, was destined for a place in the history books, not least because of its prime position right on the Solent. Alison Steele was the former Lepe Country Park Manager and is now involved with the Friends of Lepe. She frequently gives talks about the area.

More evidence of Mulberry Harbour construction at Lepe.
(Marc Heighway)

We look out across to the Island and to your right you can see the red and green posts marking the entrance to the River Beaulieu. During the war, the whole of this river estuary was requisitioned by the Navy, and there would be a constant stream of military craft going past Lepe rather than the recreational boats we can see today. A lot of the larger craft would have been stood offshore here. Smaller craft would be plying to and fro. Many of those would have been manned by WRENs who were based at nearby Beaulieu. They had to be out in all weathers; believe me, a strong south-westerly wind whistling up the Solent can produce some big waves. They had to go out sometimes at night-time, ferrying equipment out to the larger vessels and perhaps occasionally taking the odd drunken sailor back home. Just a little further along the estuary of the River Beaulieu, is Lepe House, which is one of the eleven large houses that were requisitioned locally for use by military personnel during the war. Its position here at the entrance to the river Beaulieu made it an important signals base for naval activities. Along the beach, if you were to go further you would come to Inchmery House and that was a base for training Polish and French troops.

Mention must be made again of one of the fascinating stories about this area. Depending on which source one refers to, between 6,000 and 9,000 American troops left from Lepe for Operation Overlord, and therefore it is understandable that the focal point of this country park is the magnificent Anchor memorial. A visitor, Royal Army Service Corps (RASC) veteran Fred Nicholas, commented that he found the memorial 'very moving':

They have gone to a lot of trouble to acknowledge what our generation went through. It brought back a lot of memories for me, some sad, some happy. I was extremely impressed with what I saw, and I think it is good that the public still remember for the sake of all the lads that did not come home.

A re-enactor depicts a member of the wartime Observer Corps

4

Eyes to the Skies

The role of the New Forest, specifically during the Second World War, cannot be viewed in isolation from events, developments and emergency planning which involved and affected the wider county, and indeed the country. The Forest's pivotal contribution to the D-Day campaign was made possible not just by its location, its geographical features, and its valuable natural assets, but also by the addition of expertise and specialist skills from many areas. Here is the story of one such contribution, which merits historical acknowledgement, for its major role throughout the New Forest and indeed along the south coast.

The story begins in the Weald of Kent, some 15 miles south of Maidstone, in the small town of Cranbrook, with its solid square-towered church of weathered stone and its nineteenth-century windmill. Here it was that in 1924 Major General Ashmore and the Chief Constable of Kent set up an observation post to track the course of aircraft and to report on them. There were eight similar observation posts at other sites in Kent, and they were all linked by telephone to the exchange in Cranbrook Post Office – where an upstairs room became known as the 'Centre'. Major General Ashmore CB, CMGV, MVO had been put in charge of the defences of London as far back as the autumn of 1917, and he subsequently created the London Air Defence Area (LADA). This organisation coordinated reports from coastal and inland watching posts, searchlights, gun stations, balloons, and aerodromes to the south and south-east of London, yet following the end of the First World War, the authorities lost interest in the project. The RAF, which was the most powerful service of its type in the world with 20,000 aircraft, had by March 1923 a mere three squadrons allocated to home defence. Not surprisingly it was Winston Churchill who insisted on keeping alive the intricate and specialised art of air defence. As a result of pressure by Churchill and a Committee of Inquiry report, it was agreed that 'a highly organised system is essential for the rapid collection and distribution of information and intelligence regarding the movements of hostile and friendly aircraft throughout the whole area of possible air operations'.

Following the success of the trials that involved the Cranbrook Centre and its other eight posts, it was decided to extend the system to twenty-seven posts in Kent and sixteen in Sussex, with centres in Maidstone and Horsham, respectively. In the summer of 1925 three squadrons of aircraft participated in complex simulated attacks on the capital. All were suc-

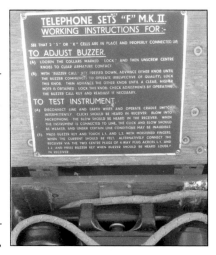

A field telephone of the type used by the ROC. This was discovered near Ringwood. (AC)

cessfully tracked and plotted. The report of the trials was accepted, and on 29 October 1925 its recommendations were put into effect, making the Observer Corps (OC) an official organisation. Following the formation of No. 1 Group in Kent and No. 2 Group in Sussex, Major General Ashmore turned his attention to the county of Hampshire, which he surveyed in the early months of 1926. Home defence was the responsibility of the War Office, which delegated local control to the chief constable of each county. It was from the ranks of special constables that the nucleus of the teams who worked in the Cranbrook Centre and at the Observation Posts (OPs) in the field, were selected. Locally, as more members were recruited, so they too became special constables, and by May 1926 Brigadier General Du Boulay CMG had been chosen as Winchester's first Controller, and a small room was provided in Winchester's post office as Hampshire's Centre.

On 1 June 1926, Major General Ashmore met his new Controller, the Chief Constable of Hampshire and some of the OC Specials at the post office in Winchester, to explain the new reporting system. No. 3 Group was created, and by the end of 1926 there were twenty-three observation and reporting sites in the county. They were linked by telephone in clusters of three to the Control Centre in Winchester, but soon space in the tiny room at the post office became a problem. In 1927, the Centre and its switchboard moved to a bigger room in a nearby store and here it remained for six years. It was then transferred to the Blue Triangle Club in Winchester, which was incidentally, the Young Women's Christian Association (YWCA) headquarters. General Du Boulay retired in 1933 and was succeeded by Colonel G.N. Salmon CMG, DSO. During his first two years, clusters of posts were added to the map, including coverage of the Isle of Wight, where four posts were established. These were located at Newport, Sandown, Niton and Freshwater. On 1 January 1929, control of the OC had been transferred from the War Office to the Air Ministry, which by then had become responsible for training, although Chief Constables were still in charge of recruiting and controlling personnel. On 8 March 1929, the Air Ministry appointed Air Commodore G.A.D. Masterman as its first Commandant.

Meanwhile, Centre personnel in their room at the YWCA in Winchester had been complaining, for some time, that dance music from the Blue Triangle Club in the same building was interfering with their duties, and so the Centre was moved once more, this time to a wooden building erected on the roof of the Post Office Telephone Exchange in Brook Street. It was from this exposed and highly vulnerable position that they participated in the August 1939 air exercises, and interestingly, in was a month later that the Corps members listened to Chamberlain's announcement that this country was at war with Germany. Just as exposed, if not more so, were the observers in the field, who were equipped with no more than a canvas screen to keep some of the draught from their legs. At the outbreak of war, each post was given £5 to build a protective structure, and many weird and wonderful creations resulted. Lockerley Green Post, near Romsey boasted a plumber, a builder, and a coal merchant among their number, and they built a splendid home from home, with rotating windscreens and central heating. This was a far cry from the bleak field and its solitary telegraph pole that they started with in 1926! Tracking by sound had been practised successfully from the early days. At no. 3/G2 Post located in Sway, near Brockenhurst in the New Forest, the Head Observer was an Engineer and a Veteran of the First World War by the name of Captain R.H.C. Ball. He took part in official plotting trials with a Vickers Virginia aircraft from RAF Worthy Down*, near Winchester. Captain Ball is also credited with the design of the standard post plotting instrument for which a Royal Observer Corps (ROC) observer, by the name of Micklethwait, later designed the height corrector.

The airfield at Worthy Down was operational from 1916 and it became RAF Worthy Down, in 1939.

The Winchester OC Centre moved again. In 1940 it transferred away from the dangerous rooftop location on the Post Office and took up residency in Northgate House in Jewry Street. Here it was to remain throughout the Battle of Britain and the busy two years following, before moving finally in 1943 to a purpose-built Operations Centre in Abbotts Road on the city outskirts. Colonel Salmon, the Controller, had been joined in 1938 by Major General Sir William Twiss KCIE, CB, CBE, MC, as Observer Group Officer, and it was he who took over as Winchester's first Group Commandant in 1943 when Colonel Salmon retired. The Winchester Group was privileged to contribute to the development of several plotting and reporting techniques, not least of which was assistance to friendly aircraft lost or in distress, a story subsequently told by Wing Commander Bulmore in his book The Dark Haven. In 1943, further aircraft reporting posts were added to the Group, which now covered not only Hampshire, the New Forest, and the Isle of Wight, but also the fringes of Sussex, Surrey, Oxfordshire, Wiltshire, and Dorset in a network of some eighty posts linked in clusters of threes and fours by telephone to the Control Centre in Winchester. It was the time of the enemy hit-and-run raider, individual pilots who flew at low level using valleys and natural features to avoid detection. The ROC rose to the challenge and introduced new and faster tracking methods. During 1943 and the early part of 1944, through what was the start of the build-up to D-Day, Hampshire and the New Forest were in the thick of it, so much so that the 'mass plot' was introduced for occasions when large formations or constant streams of aircraft, too numerous to be counted, passed over. The ROC was quite appropriately referred to as 'the eyes and ears of the RAF' because throughout the war they identified and tracked all aircraft flying over the country by day and by night. Radar beams were directed seaward to provide advance information of incoming flights, and once these aircraft could be seen from the coast they were 'handed over' to the ROC for further tracking. Information from the posts was collated at their Centres and passed to Fighter Command, which directed fighters to intercept the incoming enemy fighters and bombers and passed information on to the Air Raid warning network and other interested parties. All raids during the Battle of Britain, the London Blitz, and the big air raids on cities such as Coventry were handled in this way.

The Battle of Britain is so well documented that the details will not be repeated here. Suffice to say that the Corps was justifiably proud of the part it played in the battle, and official recognition came on 9 April 1941, when it was announced in Parliament that 'in recognition of the valuable services rendered by the Observer Corps over

The site of a former ROC post at Ipley Cross. (Marc Heighway)

a number of years, His Majesty the King has been graciously pleased to approve that the Corps shall henceforth be known by the style and description of The Royal Observer Corps'.

The amphibious landings at Dieppe on 19 August 1942, although a disaster, highlighted several lessons to be learnt, one of which was that many Allied planes were being shot down by our own gunners. This prompted Air Vice Marshal Sir Trafford Leigh-Mallory KCB, DSO, RAF, then commanding 11 Group, to suggest that naval gunners should be trained in aircraft recognition. He went on to suggest that ROC personnel would be suitable for this task. Although the use of the ROC was rejected by the Air Ministry, the need for men skilled in aircraft recognition to be carried on ships was recognised. Subsequent losses of Allied planes from friendly fire generally, and specifically at the landings at Salerno and Sicily, only served to emphasise the need.

As planning for the invasion of occupied Europe got under way, it became apparent that the aircraft recognition experts already in the Services, namely RAF aircrew and certain anti-aircraft units in the Army were going to be otherwise engaged. Air Chief Marshal Leigh-Mallory's suggestion of employing members of the ROC as aircraft identifiers was therefore resurrected and subsequently adopted. Thus, what was known as the Seaborne project, whereby members of the Royal Observer Corps took part in the invasion of Europe, came about. While the 'Seabornes' were away, the first V1 flying bombs were sighted (13 June 1944), and they continued to rain down for many more months until 29 March 1945, when their launch sites in France and Holland were finally overrun. Almost all were targeted on London. To meet this new threat, some Observers were drafted to help man the posts in and around London. Once again, the Corps played a considerable and mostly unsung part in the defeat of the V1s. They were less effective against the V2s, but then the whole of the defence system was seemingly powerless against them. More than 1,000 were plotted between 8 September 1944 and 27 March 1945, and their sites of impact were reported.

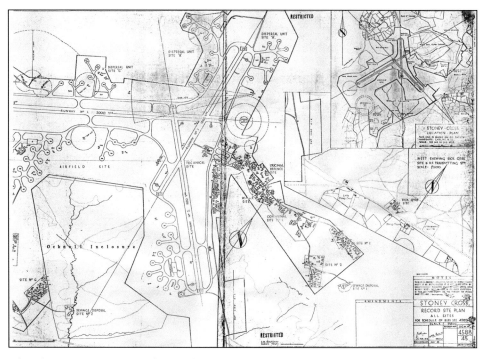

The Observer Corps operated in tandem with local airfields such as Stoney Cross. (NARA Archives)

Forward Aircraft Observation Posts (FAOP) were created at the following locations in the New Forest:

Barton (Specialist Satellite Post or SSP)	Lyndhurst
Christchurch	Marchwood
Copythorne (the site is now buried	New Milton
beneath the M27 motorway)	Ringwood
Exbury	Sway
Fordingbridge	Verwood
Hengistbury (SSP)	Boscombe/New Milton
Keyhaven (SSP)	

Evidence of some of these sites is still visible, but please check with the ROC Museum (see reference section). The role they played was one of vital support, particularly during 1943 and in the months up to and including D-Day.

By the spring of 1945, the end of the war was in sight. German air raids were sporadic and generally restricted to low-level hit-and-run attacks on airfields and the like, and some reconnaissance flights were being made by the enemy's new Arado 234B jets. The ROC stood down on 12 May 1945, just four days after Victory in Europe (VE) Day. There was much clearing up to be done and several end-of-war parades to take part in, but of course the full-time men and women were now out of a job. The 1945 Birthday Honours List and the 1946 New Year Honours List contained the names of 60 personnel who between them were awarded four OBEs (Order of the British Empire), fourteen MBEs (Member of the Order of the British Empire) and forty-two BEMs (British Empire Medal) in final recognition of the war service of the ROC.

A small cadre of officers was maintained at ROC Headquarters and caretaker officers were appointed to every Group and Area. It was soon realised that there would be a peacetime role for the ROC, and after eighteen months in limbo the call went out for the Corps to recommence training.

On parade, the wartime Fire Service in Hampshire (HFRS)

5

On Manoeuvres

Often written about in past centuries as the 'Threshold of Ocean and Empire', the port of Southampton has always played its part in the life of the nation, both in times of peace and of war. Its role during the Second World War was pivotal and thankfully that history is well documented. On the north-western outskirts of the city is the community of Totton which also played its part in the war effort, and whilst not immediately on the front line in the same way as its larger neighbour, Totton hosted a vital service that helped to fight the war on the Home Front.

An early twentieth-century traveller wrote:
Beyond Totton for the first miles, a stranger may be forgiven both impatience and the question, 'Where is the Forest?', but gradually the orderly ordinariness of the road grows less, and after the railway is crossed at Lyndhurst Road, one might be passing through a very spacious and somewhat unkempt park, yet this is indeed the Forest.

Totton is on the edge of the Forest and is clustered around the main arterial routes into the area, one from Southampton (the A33), from Salisbury (the A326), whilst the A36 takes the visitor through the town centre. Testwood Lane leads to Testwood Sports College, a relatively new name for Testwood School, which opened on this site in 1946. Take a moment to observe the older parts of the school, which belie its immediate pre-war utilitarian style. The building at Testwood was requisitioned by the government and pressed into service for the war effort. It was to become a regional training centre for National Fire Service (NFS) personnel, and in 1942, under the auspices of the NFS, it welcomed men of the Canadian Corps of Fire Fighters (also known as the Civilian Corps of Canadian Fire Fighters), who were volunteers drawn from military and civilian fire brigades throughout Canada.

Canadian firefighters on pump drill (AC)

The little-known story of the 406 firemen who served in England between 1942 and 1945 is as fascinating as it is inspiring. Having given up their safe existence in Canada to travel through U-boat-infested waters to an uncertain future helping fight fires on the Home Front, these volunteers excelled in their duties and left a lasting impression on all those with whom they served and met during their time in England.

Just two years from its mobilisation in September 1939, the peacetime Fire Service had, despite many operational problems and other related difficulties, met the challenges thrust upon it by war. The peacetime strength of some 50,000 personnel had expanded, in its new civil defence role, from 200,000 at the outbreak of war to about 300,000 by the spring of 1941. The core strength comprised regular firemen, volunteers, part-timers, and members of the Auxiliary Fire Service. In addition, there were stirrup parties, as well as various supplementary fire-fighting groups, including those employed by private estates in the New Forest. However, there was a need for more help. Bombing of English cities continued, and although there was a brief lull, in mid-1941 further significant attacks took place on London. The Fire Service had now been nationalised. A renewed call for assistance went out from the British government, and further consideration was given to the formation of a Canadian fire-fighting unit to serve in the United Kingdom.

CANADIAN PERSONNEL 2Z STATION
SOUTHAMPTON 1943

Canadian firemen based in Southampton helped to carry out trials on PLUTO at Lepe (AC)

Various meetings took place between and within the British and Canadian governments, when matters including pay, pension, benefits, transportation, recruitment, finance, and equipment for, and the actual status of, the firefighters were discussed at length. From 24 June 1942 and for several months thereafter, a total of 406 volunteers in several contingents arrived in the United Kingdom, and after training and familiarisation at Testwood (and Ivybridge in Devon), units were posted to major cities including London, Southampton, and Portsmouth.

The late Cyril Kendall of Totton was an officer in the NFS: 'The Canadians donated thousands of feet of rubber hose which became known, not surprisingly as Canadian Hose. That was one of the best things that ever happened, getting all that hose which fitted, and with the addition of our connectors could be used anywhere.'

Jack Coulter served with the Corps of Canadian Fire Fighters. During his time in the Corps, he became a Leading Fire Fighter. On a visit to England in the early 2000's he recorded that:
We arrived in Liverpool after nine days at sea. Our ship, the Dominion Monarch, had been part-converted into a troop ship. Yes, I lived on bread and cheese and jam for the entire journey. The mutton they offered me was simply not edible.
Immediately upon arrival, we were put on a train for Southampton, and from there

we were transported to Testwood, just outside the city in a district called Totton. The grounds had been converted into a training facility for the National Fire Service.
We learnt really quick, the techniques of the different trailer pumps and hydrants, and the fact that air raids often destroyed the water mains. In the city, there were large steel and concrete tanks full of water, and in some cases, basements of buildings were used for water storage. We were often called to travel to other locations and one time we went to Bournemouth where we spent two weeks after one raid. Home for us was the Alliance Hotel, near the docks in Southampton.

Jack Coulter at Testwood Totton (AC)

Detachment 1 was sent to Southampton and arrived there in August 1942, with the men being divided between the stations in Hulse Road and Marsh Lane, commanded by Chief Officer Thornton and Chief Officer Scott, respectively. In this city, the Canadians helped with the provision of static water tanks, and later assisted the NFS during the trials of the PLUTO pipeline at Lepe.

The late Tom Porter, who was serving as a member of the NFS, recalled:
I first met the Canadians when our National Fire Service unit was moved to Testwood. We had always drawn most of our vehicle fuel from Testwood before we were transferred there, although we also had access to a pump on a local garage forecourt, and when the Canadians arrived, we went with them to draw fuel from the garage.

Mary Belbin, an NFS firewoman from Totton, remembered:
The Canadians came to Southampton, I do not know how many, but there were quite a few. They used to tell us about their families because I suppose they were homesick, which is quite understandable, but also it helped us to get to know them better and they became part of our big family.

Jennifer Turner (née Powell) of Waterside, Hampshire recalled:
When I was young, about eighteen, I took up the offer of going to local dances with

one of the Canadians. I am sorry, but I cannot remember his name. All the men I met were good to me as a young person and they gave me small gifts, usually consisting of some of their rations, which included sweets. My mother said that they used to talk a lot about their families and that they always acted like real gentlemen. I believe some of the men used to get invited to people's homes for meals, but I cannot be sure. I know that one of the firemen was killed in the city,

Mary Belbin (second right) and a friend with two of the Canadian Firefighters (AC)

(Southampton), but I only found that out after the war when the story was told to me by an aunt.

Off duty, the Canadians excelled at team competitions at the Testwood site. Jack Coulter again:

We had a tow vehicle and trailer pump and we had to drive forward to a tank. The idea was to disconnect the pump from the truck then get the suction in the water of the tank, lay the hose out and knock down a target with the jet of water. This was a fairly standard type of competition. We Canadians, probably being a little younger and a little more active than the British, were able to compete well and we became the winners of the competition. As a result, we were presented with a trophy. All this was filmed by a crew from Canada working for the National Film Board.

Mary Belbin wrote:

We used to have field [sports] days and for that I used to wear my best uniform. We went and served teas from the mobile kitchen that had been donated by the Canadian Red Cross.

Tom Porter also remembers field days attended by the Canadians:

The thing that struck me was the strength of these men. They were very strong and could pick up a light pump off its trailer and carry it without any trouble. There were handles on the end for the British firemen to lift the pump. Also, another thing that struck me was the way they handled fire gear. When they ran out a hose, they never carried the branch (hose) under their arm like we did. They just threw it from one man to the next a bit like throwing a baseball.

The Canadians were often to be seen travelling from Totton to Lepe beach and to Hatchett's Pond, where they carried out various training exercises. As Jack Walters wrote in his book (published in 1977), 'The local division of the Auxiliary Fire Service, later the NFS, for example, used Hatchett's Pond for training purposes; so too did the RAF who carried out simulated rescue exercises for Aircrews.' Distinguished by their larger build and noted for the thigh-high protective service boots they wore, the Canadians proved to be a popular addition to the multinational wartime community of the New Forest. Their popularity was further enhanced when in early 1943 Leading Fireman Bryce, serving alongside his brother who had also volunteered for service in England, responded to cries for help. A child was in difficulties in the River Test and was in danger of drowning. Without a thought for his own safety, Bryce was quick to jump into action and managed to save the child's life. For this brave act, he was awarded the Humane Medal.

During their service on Britain's Home Front, the Canadians suffered five casualties and three deaths. Fireman 'Scotty' Coull, number T112 of Winnipeg, died in July 1944, a casualty of a flying bomb attack. He is laid to rest in Lossiemouth, Scotland and at his burial he was given full military honours. Local people contributed towards the cost of his headstone. Section Leader Lawrence 'Curly' Woodhead, number T305 from Saskatoon, died in June 1944 when he fell from a speeding fire engine during a training exercise in Southampton.

Mary Belbin again:
They used to go out on manoeuvres and sometimes the fire engines were overloaded with men. One of the firemen fell off the lorry and was killed. They put his coffin in the hall at Testwood and it was draped with the Canadian flag. We all went down to pay our respects.

Section Leader Alfred LaPierre, number T212 of Montreal, was killed in Bristol, and with Lawrence Woodhead was laid to rest with full military honours in the grounds of the Canadian section of Brookwood Cemetery in Woking, Surrey.

The Canadian volunteers served until the end of the war. They saw service during the Blitz and were involved in various activities in the New Forest and Hampshire in support of the preparations for the D-Day landings. A fine commemorative plaque in their memory was unveiled at a high-profile ceremony, attended by representatives from the Canadian Government in 2008 at Hampshire Fire and Rescue Service Headquarters, Leigh Road, Eastleigh Hampshire. Viewing of the plaque may be possible by contacting HFRS.

The memorial plaque to the Canadian Firefghters at HFRS Eastleigh

*Heavy equipment seen preparing the site at Stoney Cross Airfield
(Authors Collection)*

6

Defending the Realm

The Home Guard was ready for action, ingenious positions known as Stop Lines were introduced as part of the countrywide plan to create a strategy of defence in the event of invasion and supported by the WAAFs, the men of the RAF provided the line of defence in the skies.

Bernard Job joined the Royal Air Force Volunteer Reserve in June 1942, following acceptance for aircrew duties. He was nineteen years of age.

'*At the initial Training Wing it was decided that I was suitable navigator material and so I, with many others like me, embarked on the long training process, both in this country and in Canada. I was commissioned and finally gained my Observers Brevet in September 1943. The N, navigator brevet was officially introduced shortly afterwards. I then joined the Operational Training Unit at Greenwood, Nova Scotia where we flew in Mosquito aircraft for the first time. It was much more exciting than the navigation training Anson's that we had flown in up to then. We were also crewed up with our pilots all of whom had been specially selected to fly this particular aircraft, the Mosquito.*

I was crewed with Flying Officer, later Flight Lieutenant Jack Phillips of the Canadian Air Force. In time we flew back to England and did further and more exacting training at the Mosquito Operational Training Unit at High Ercall in Shropshire'.

Bernard was then sent to an airfield in the south of England.
It was April 1944 that I travelled south and eventually stepped off the train at Hinton Admiral Halt, near Christchurch where I was greeted by a WAAF driver. She was

waiting to take me to Holmsley South, which would be my first operational station. Things were going to be rather different from then on. My friend, Jack Phillips and I were members of 418 City of Edmonton Squadron, Royal Canadian Air Force. Almost all the pilots were from Canada other than the Squadron Commander, Wing Commander Tony Barker who was career Royal Air Force. There was a fair sprinkling of RAF VR Navigators

Bernard Job and Jack Phllips at Holmsley (AC)

too and one Jamaican, Frank Smith was his name, amongst the crews.

Holmsley was in 11th Group of Fighter Command and, with a very few other Squadrons, classified as a night intruder Squadron. We had Mk VI Mosquito's the fighter/ bomber variant equipped with four 20mm cannon and four Browning machine guns. They could also carry two 500 lb bombs when necessary. The Squadrons main task at that time was to surprise and intercept enemy aircraft over their airfields at night and to, shall we say, generally disrupt enemy airfield activity.

Given the opportunity, yes, we attacked ground targets. No airborne radar, known as A.I. (Aircraft Interception) was available at the time, but despite this, the Squadron had already achieved a creditable record of kills during operations over enemy territory, mainly at night. The usual pattern when Ops were on was the night flying test in daylight hours to check serviceability and later, when targets or patrol areas had been allocated by Group, flight planning and pre-flight briefing. Crews were given considerable flexibility in determining and routing to target areas - a privilege extended to very, very few other Squadrons. Most operations were carried out at low level, little more than normal circuit height in fact. Good visibility was essential for the job and so reasonable weather conditions were crucial. Navigation was decidedly basic with an accurate flight plan followed by dead reckoning and the limited map reading possible using major landmarks, for example rivers over the darkened continent, all which really had to suffice. What was called the G Hyperbolic Navigation System was very new and only helpful to us within range nearer home.

Squadron morale under Wing Commander Barker was high and after a few familiarisation flights we did our first patrol. Other Operations followed, usually to enemy airfields in France. During this part of the Operation Overlord, that is the build up to D Day, Squadron aircraft were in action just before the landings for bombing airfields and covering some of the parachute drops which occurred.

Once the Allied Landings in Normandy had been accomplished, 418 Squadron aircraft stepped up their operations in France in order to suppress German night fighter activity against our bombers.

The French airfields meantime had been considerably reinforced and our aircraft often met intensive flak and persistent searchlight coning. The latter was sometimes countered by the decidedly dangerous tactic of diving down the beam and dousing the installation with canon fire.

Very soon a new threat appeared in the shape of the V1 missiles which were extremely fast, pulse jet propelled bombs, dubbed by the public, Doodlebugs or Buzz Bombs. They were, however, no laughing matter and were causing many civilian casualties in and around London and the South-East. So, 418 Squadron then took on the additional task of what were called "Anti-Diver patrols" over the English Channel at night. Diver was, incidentally, the military code name for the V1. There were two kinds of operation involved and these were firstly, direct attacks on any V1's seen. They had a very visible exhaust trail so could be spotted fairly easily. Operation two was using spotter patrols to identify the launch sites in the Pas de Calais area so that bombers could be sent in later.

Downing the V1's in flight proved difficult when attempted at low level because at about 400 Mph they were able to outrun the Mk VI Mosquito, which did something like a maximum of 350 mph at sea level.

So it was that Squadron Leader Russ Bannock RCAF, who later became Wing Commander and Commanding Officer of the Squadron, and Squadron Leader Don MacFadyer evolved an attack strategy of patrolling at 10,000 ft and diving steeply to intercept whilst accelerating to about 430 Mph. This meant that an interception proved highly successful and altogether the Squadron shot down 80 V1's in the period until August 1944 when the launch sites were overrun by the advancing allied armies. During this time there were many tales of having to avoid and sometimes bring back to base some of the debris which usually resulted from the initial disintegration of the V1 target at close range before it went into the sea and the explosive charge was triggered.

418 Squadron left Holmsley South for nearby Hurn on the 13[th of] July 1944 and then, quite soon afterwards they moved to Middle Wallop near Andover, Hampshire. But throughout all this the normal pattern of night intruding went on, sometimes deep into Germany and the tally of aircraft kills increased with, luckily, relatively few losses ourselves. By the time 418 Squadron was transferred out of Fighter Command into Second Tactical Air Force in November 1944 the score sheet of No 418 Squadron totalled some 178 aircraft destroyed including 105 in the air. Thereafter their operations were in support of the Allied armies on the ground with rather more bombing sorties mostly at night and at low level.

Looking back, the former 418 crew members remember some of the good times at Holmsley South as well as the bad, when things went sadly wrong. For example, when they made a count after a series of sorties and found they were missing friends who were not to be seen again. That was very upsetting, but as Bernard said,
We had to pull ourselves together and got on with what we had to do. There was no time for grieving.

The Cat and Fiddle pub, which today is still a very popular meeting place on the main A35 road between Lyndhurst and Christchurch was, for example, a popular venue when crews had been stood down for the night. Occasional horse riding in the Forest was memorable, particularly for those like Bernard who admitted that he found it hard to stay in the saddle.

On the airfield the daytime flying discipline of rocket equipped Typhoon Wing also stationed there was quite impressive. The occasional crash on take-off reminded us of the vulnerability of these Napier engine aircraft. We were forever thankful that we had the incomparable Rolls Royce Merlin's in the Mosquito. Operationally, there were many times when plans went wrong, and we had to extricate ourselves from trouble. On a daylight sortie to engage Luftwaffe aircraft on the Baltic coast, we had to abort when we were hit by intense anti-aircraft fire over the Danish coast. We limped home to base thanks mainly to my pilot who was seriously wounded (I suffered only minor shrapnel wounds). We were together again on operations just three months later.

Another kind of experience was the one we had one night over enemy occupied Holland during a storm in which we encountered St Elmo's fire. With our navigation lights on and off and our props two circles of fire, we felt pretty exposed for a time. But we got through it and survived! All in all, the same team, Jack Phillips, and I, completed 44 sorties on 418 squadron.

A surviving pillbox at former RAF Calshot (Marc Heighway)

In support of the Royal Air Force were the wonderful women of the WAAF (Women's Auxiliary Air Force). Doris Paice left the shores of England in 1948 for new adventures and a different way of life in New Zealand. Sharing her memories from the other side of the world, during the early years of the 21st century, Doris recalled the war years with mixed emotions.

I served in Coastal Command and initially I was based on the west coast of England, but then I was transferred to the station at RAF Calshot at the southern tip of Southampton water in Hampshire. This was well known as a seaplane base and was very much part of the country's aviation history. The flying boat sheds I remember of course because they were huge and today, I believe one of them remains as a well-known landmark. Calshot was also one of the main centres for the Air Sea Rescue Boats.

The Commanding Officer there was one of the old school, and I believe he was the Commodore of the RAF Yacht Squadron during peacetime. He was extremely interested in yachting anyway and knew really everything about charts and so on. I was one of the chart girls and my trade was Clerk/GD/Maps responsible for correcting Admiralty Charts from the publications that were being issued by the Admiralty to all Sunderland bases and Air Sea Rescue units. You have to realise that with so much disruption everywhere the navigation channels for ships and so on were changing all the time. The Admiralty was putting out changes to the charts every week for simple things like changes to the lighting on buoys, shifting sands and the movement of lightships to identifying mined areas and all the wrecks as well. Here of course the charts were used by the Air Sea Rescue lads and by the seaplanes and flying boats because their crews needed to know where it was OK to touch down as well as knowing if they were flying over 'safe' water.

Calshot has a long history because of the old castle which is right on the spit. Before the Second World War it was a peace time base and the WAAFs were billeted in what used to be the married quarters. They were allocated rooms which accommodated three WAAFS and apparently it was very comfortable, considering the age of the buildings and the fact they were on a very exposed promontory.

There was a small railway which ran the length of the spit because the whole area was part of the establishment. At the western end there was the old officers club and at the eastern side was the main centre and the waterside activities. The train with its small wooden coaches was out of bounds for the airmen, but the WAAFS were allowed to use it to travel to the Chart Offices. Riding on the train was always a novelty and just something different and something Doris remembers as part of the experiences of the war she and her comrades 'shared' at Calshot.

I also remember that the Commanding Officer used to spend a lot of time in the chart room with the WAAFS, or the chart girls as we were known. It was unusual for a senior officer to spend so much time with the other ranks, but he was always passing on his knowledge and he seemed to like the business of charting and navigation. We considered it something of a privilege that he wanted to pass on what he knew, but I think it was for this reason that we were not very popular on the base because we were known as the Commanding Officers 'darling's'. We could not do anything wrong, and we did lead rather a charmed life as you might say. At the time I don't suppose we considered this anything other than normal but looking back I suppose we did get out of a lot of the more routine jobs and things like drill. The work was interesting and because it was shift work there were twenty of us to cover around the clock. I used to cycle off base a lot because like all RAF stations, there were always bicycles available from the official store and providing you signed them in and out, there was never any problem borrowing a bike.

There was no public transport to speak of and cars were not available to us, so I used to cycle out around the new Forest whenever the opportunity occurred. I went up to

Beaulieu and across to Lyndhurst, places I still remember to this day. It was so peaceful and sometimes despite the sight of military vehicles and people in uniform, it was difficult to believe there was a war.

Doris was posted to Chivenor in North Devon for a short time, but she returned to Calshot and was there when hostilities ended in Europe in May 1944.

I did move around with Coastal Command between my stints at Calshot and was based in Stranraer, Blackpool, Carlisle, and Turnberry. Needless to say, that when the end came everybody went quite silly for a while and the relief was hard to describe. I know we had a huge bonfire at Calshot and part of the old train, well the wooden carriages, went on the fire. Some of the men burnt furniture as well. It was mad here and I am told that everybody was having a really good time in nearby Southampton too. Lots of people got really drunk but who can blame them?

At wars end, Doris had been in the Women's Auxiliary Air Force for about five and a half years. When she went home on leave, she soon realised that she was leading the good life by comparison to those in civvy street. She says she ate well, put on weight, and enjoyed good rations. She was able to save her cigarettes and sweets allowances and take them home to her family.

We had chocolates in our rations, and we did well because the portions at home were meagre. I had sisters, two were in the Land Army and one in the Auxiliary Territorial Service, (ATS). My mother and father and elder sister all smoked heavily so they had my cigarette rations.

There was never much in the shops, no meat, clothes, groceries and so on. There were hard times for the folk on the Home Front. When I was in the services I was in my own little world, as we all were on camp, and you really didn't have much of an idea as to what was going on around you. I served from 1941 to 1946 so quite a stint really, but it was very enjoyable and an experience that you cannot sufficiently describe to the younger generations.

I do not regret one day of my service and the small part I played in helping the war effort and the eventual outcome of good winning over evil.

Elsa Hastings, Women's Auxiliary Air Force, (WAAF) was posted to Beaulieu Airfield:

We were billeted in huts near the airfield. When we first joined the WAAFs, our smart uniforms and doing our bit for the war effort made us feel really very proud, but in the winter when we were chipping the ice off water buckets so we could get water to wash in, we did wonder what we had let ourselves in for. Conditions when we were at Calshot were better however, looking back I am glad I was able to do my small bit despite everything.

From diary notes,

Dad and my young brother went to the camp at Stoney to ask if they had any food leftovers to feed our pigs.

Elsa Hastings WAAF, for a time stationed at both Beaulieu and Calshot stations (E.Hastings)

The Americans knew that we were on rations and many people found it a struggle to cope so sometimes they were able to get meat from their PX canteen which they wrapped up securely and left for us to collect from their kitchen swill bin.

Many Forest people used a pony and trap to get around in those days. After the war, huts on the airfields were available to rent and our family had friends at the old Ibsley airfield and some other friends at Holmsley. The children used to play all over the sites which were still quite built up with the original control towers and so on. There were also Army Huts around and people I think who had been bombed out from the cities moved in. I can't recall if the huts had electricity, but the families made them quite habitable and quiet snug as best they could. Over the years, new homes were being built and as families moved out the huts became derelict and eventually all were moved out and the sites were either turned back to agriculture or used for other purposes.

Chris Lewis lived near New Milton and recalled that,

My father was in the local Home Guard, and I often went with them as they patrolled the local area presumably looking for enemy paratroopers or shot-down aircrew. I cannot remember them ever finding anything other than vast amounts of the metallic chaff known as 'window' that was dropped by aircraft to confuse ground radar. For some unknown reason, our larder contained lots of this chaff still in thick wads that had not broken up in the air as it was supposed to. I cannot imagine what my father intended to do with it, but he did tend to hoard things that might come in useful one day. I know that we had bombs dropped in the general area, but I think that death or injury from dropping lumps of chaff would have been more likely here'

Southern Home Guard Camouflage instruction (Hampshire History Home Guard)

The Home Guard served their local villages and towns very well and as time passed, they were held in greater esteem. Tom Watson in Bournemouth saw the Home Guard in action, particularly when firing at low flying enemy 'planes.

They stood in place without flinching and shot off round after round at the Messerschmitt's which were flying low and machine-gunning everything in sight.

Across the region, preparations for possible invasion, either by sea or air, or both, were considered the priority. It was considered, for example, that the main threat to the Hampshire/Dorset border region was an enemy force, landing on the south coast and using the Avon valley, along the route of the A338, as an axis of advance inland. Here, as elsewhere, 'stop lines' were created through the emplacement of pillboxes, the creation of fortifications, preparations for the use of anti-tank rails and roadblocks and the training and equipping of the legendary 'underground Army'.

The objective of what was to be known, in this case, as the Ringwood stop line was to deny east-west movement, and vice versa, and presumably the use of the A338.

The two channels of the River Avon are between 45 and 90 feet in width and in 1940 would have presented quite an obstacle for an invading force. The fast-flowing water is deep and there are irrigation channels with steep sides and although there is a bridge to cross each channel, they are quite narrow. However, a single-track railway ran north- south, just 600 feet from the water mill at Breamore and this line would have been very easy to cross for any lightly mechanised force.

The crossing point at Breamore, near Fordingbridge, was defended and fortified as part of a network of fortifications to cover both possibilities, attack from the west (the A338), and attack from the east. Part of the stop line defence can still be seen today and its worthy of some study to those interested in how the country would have attempted the defence of the realm in the 1940's. Three pillboxes provided almost 360-degree coverage of the crossing point. The first pillbox, situated right on the bank of the river, is a modified Type 26, of concrete and brick and it was emplaced to cover the Breamore to Woodgreen road from the west. Part of the blast wall was removed, and this was possibly, to enhance the field of fire from one embrasure. Faded red paint suggests that attempts were made to camouflage the structure because it would have been a logical step to make it blend in with surrounding buildings, all of which are of natural brick. Effective fire from this emplacement and the exposed approach would make access by the enemy, an extremely hazardous exercise. Pillbox two which is also a Type 26, is on the north-east corner of Breamore Mill and was sited to cover the open area across the water meadows and the

Left: A surviving hutment at former RAF Beaulieu (Marc Heighway)
Right: More evidence of former RAF Calshot (Marc Heighway)

Breamore to Woodgreen road. However, the third emplacement is totally unique to the site, having been built in part of the mill outbuilding. Unlike pillboxes one and two, this emplacement is extremely well camouflaged and is not immediately obvious to the passer by. The position of the mill and pillboxes, on what is a small island area within the channels of the river, provided good observation and defence potential.

So, to the passer-by then, even today, there is no obvious indication as to the former importance of the site. One's attention is drawn to the 'chocolate box' facade of the mill building and the rushing waters of the Avon. It is only upon much closer inspection that the 'gun slits' become obvious.

The Type 26 pillbox was one design of 12 standard pillboxes built for the War Office Directorate of Fortifications. The modified versions at Breamore are not unusual in that across the country, local variations were made to standard designs and some structures were purpose built. Types 22 and 24 are usually sited on roadsides, and the Type 27 was often located on or near airfields. The larger Type 28, with walls some 3-foot thick, held a 2 pounder anti-tank gun.

Fortunately, this stop line was never used in an invasion scenario and it is pure conjecture as to how effective it would have been in full operational conditions.

(See elsewhere in this book references to Breamore and the Stop Line)

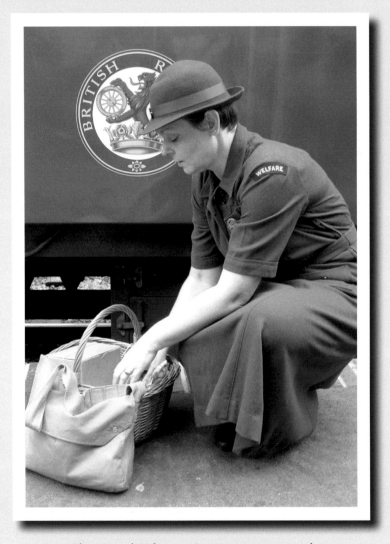

*The Women's Voluntary Service was an essential
part of wartime daily life.*

7

They Also Served

Tea, buns, a listening ear, and a lot more besides. The dedicated service of thousands of women in local communities became synonymous with the 'essence' of life on the Home Front and the 'spirit' that helped to win the War.

The Land Army was present in Hampshire and in the New Forest in great numbers, helping on the farms and estates and wherever else there was a need to tend the land and get involved in animal husbandry. The work was hard, the hours were long, but as one former Land Army member said, 'the camaraderie was strong'. The Timber Corps, including those based at the key New Forest site at Holmsley, on the A35 between Lyndhurst and Hinton Admiral, helped to maintain the constant supply of wood for various aspects of wartime construction and manufacture.

Here though we consider the contribution made extensively throughout the area by another organisation which was created in the late 1930s. When it became apparent to the enlightened few in Government, that there was to be a war in the 'foreseeable future' the then Home Secretary, Sir Samuel Hoare, already deeply involved with the business of Air Raid Precautions, perceived there to be a need for women volunteers to assist with associated work. Given the fact that the British were reluctant to consider unpleasant situations such as another war and given that the possibility of air attacks on the country was not making enough people sit up and take notice, Hoare wanted to recruit a force of women to help achieve 1 million volunteers who would be put 'on standby'. So it was that in 1938 Hoare approached The Dowager Marchioness of Reading who was well known for her considerable experience of charity work. Having previously made urgent telephone calls, to various personal contacts, Hoare eventually got in touch with Lady Reading, at her London home.

Hoare had discovered that existing organisations for women were not suitable as recruitment agents for a new force of women volunteers to assist the ARP, either because of some political or practical reason. His question was, 'Do you think you could start something special?' Lady Reading in reply, questioned whether she was the right person for the job, but she was assured by the Home Secretary that at the very least, he wanted her advice.

Hard at work on the land, members of the WLA (Nick Halling)

While on holiday, which began just a couple of days after her conversation with Hoare, Lady Reading produced a memorandum in which she had set out the suggested terms and guidelines for a new service to meet the challenges thrust upon it by a war. In the communiqué was the recommendation that the Home Office should provide office space, some financial assistance for clerical work and training, soon after enrolment. She believed that getting the organisation set up in such a manner that the women volunteers felt that it 'belonged to them', was paramount. She was only too well aware that the established practice of some organisations, was to utilise snobbery and patronage to secure the desired results and she could not envisage this being of any benefit to the new service. The aims of the organisation were grouped under five main headings which addressed the identified purpose and remits, and which reflected the activities of the established ARP. Clearly tasking the organisation with enrolling women into the ARP services to mobilisation strength, the new service would 'bring home' to all women, especially housewives, what air raids mean and what they can do for their families and for themselves.

The country was to be divided into regions, each with a Regional Officer who would be responsible for getting in touch with all local authorities preparing ARP schemes. Women recruits would be responsible to the local authorities and would receive training and necessary exercises from that authority. Successful completion of the various training courses would be recognised by certification, and proficiency would merit a 'distinctive sign' such as a scarf'. It is interesting to note that during the consultation and fact-finding exercise for the new service, information was sought from foreign embassies in London about the role of women in other countries. Much was learnt from Spain as to the work done by women during the Civil War and the Russian Embassy advised the enquirers that women did the same work as men in the Soviet Union. The new service was, after some deliberation, to be called the Women's Voluntary Service (for ARP) and the name was officially revealed on June 18th, 1938. Although they could enlist as ARP Wardens, it was felt that women did not have the physical endurance necessary to sustain the required level of operation during heavy raid conditions! The role of women in the ARP was therefore restricted to that of 'trainer' with the task of emphasising the need for basic ARP skills and personal training of women in the home. They were also recruited as ambulance drivers and assistants, and many joined the newly formed Transport Department as convoy drivers.

By the time war was declared, some nineteen different jobs were available to WVS volunteers and training was extensive with over eight hundred courses being arranged in London alone. The Minister of Health had already requested information from the WVS as to how many bottles of water and milk and how many escorts would be needed to evacuate cities like London and these needs were to be met when the call came. When the agreed 24 hours' notice was given for evacuation, twelve telegrams were sent from HQ to Regional Administrators including those responsible for the New Forest, and they in turn contacted Centre, District and Village Representatives. By using this simple yet effective protocol, nationally some 120,000 women were alerted and of these, seventeen thousand acted as escorts on the first evacuation.

It is true to say that locally, through no fault of the WVS, expected numbers of evacuees allocated to specific areas were either under quota or far in excess of the numbers expected and often billets prepared for expectant mothers for example, were taken by school children and vice versa. Given the vast exercise of moving people around the area, it's not surprising that in the planning process, a few mistakes were made, but these were quickly resolved by the resourcefulness of WVS members who were in a class of their own when it came to improvisation. Once in situ, evacuees had to be provided with clothing, health care, social welfare, and other support, all of which the women of the WVS attended to without so much as a blink of an eye. Centres, including those in, Brockenhurst, Lymington and Christchurch, became

Clothing Depots, Medical Centres, Billeting Offices, and Information Bureaux with members adapting as the challenges arose. Every aspect of day- to-day life was built on the solid platform of the local WVS Centre and its willing members. In addition, member's provided lending libraries, social events, receiving nurseries, furniture and repairs, toys for the children and communal feeding centres.

Later they were to extend their services further, as the Forest Airfields and numerous bases and camps became operational. Through the provision of a NAAFI style facility which used both static and mobile canteens, they served hot and cold food as well as providing chocolate, razors, and cosmetics for members of the British and Allied Services. The biggest single item of all was cigarettes. An average of over five million cigarettes were distributed every month via WVS canteens and hostels. The canteen facility was also used to considerable effect as part of a plan to assist the psychological needs of the evacuated population. In an act of what can only be described as a true understanding of people and humanity, the WVS were quick to respond to problems experienced by evacuees, host families and visiting parents.

Evacuation was to give rise to many previously unforeseen challenges and immediate action was needed to meet those challenges and to create as close to a 'normal' and stable home life as possible. However, one aspect of evacuation was to become a serious 'irritant' to host families. While most hosts were happy to welcome visits from the parents of evacuated children, they became quite alarmed by some parents who would arrive on the doorstep expecting to be fed, accommodated, and entertained for the day or weekend at the expense of the host. There was also the extra 'burden' of becoming involved in family disputes and typically this would be either the pleas of the child to be taken home or when evacuees were forthright in telling their parents that they never wanted to go home because life was better where they were. The latter was usually true in cases where children had come from an abusive or very poor family and were to realise the benefits of building a new life with their host parents, many of whom incidentally were asking if permanent fostering was possible.

And so, the idea of opening a canteen for the use of parents and evacuees during weekend visits was to prove immediately successful. Not only was the canteen regarded as neutral ground, away from the home of the host family, but it was also a good place for visiting parents to meet and talk with WVS and other agency representatives about 'problems' and to request help with various domestic and personal issues. Canteens also took away from host families the responsibility of entertaining and feeding the few thoughtless parents who always expected 'everything for free'.

A mobile laundry service was provided in local communities by the WVS. (Archive Concorde)

People from almost every social and environmental background were 'thrown' together and provided with accommodation either in a hostel or with families who were living in the 'safe' areas and who enjoyed a 'different way of life'. A child from an inner-city slum for example, might be taken in by a farming family. This would prove to be either a delight to the child or so boring that the youngster might want to take to their heels and flee at the first opportunity. The authorities responsible for evacuation had not fully realised that there was a fundamental difference between the outlook and lifestyle of people who lived in poor districts of evacuated towns and cities and those of the average country householders. Much improvisation was called for at the beginning of the evacuation scheme although this led to considerable problems, many of which landed in the laps of various WVS groups.

The WVS within its widening remit would provide help, guidance, and assistance to everyone who needed it. Pat Rouse (nee Younger) of Southampton recalls

I was told by my mum that the WVS helped to clothe us when we were bombed out from Southampton and they organised new accommodation and contacted family members in Bransgore, who provided us with safety in the country. I also apparently had a couple of small toys given by the WVS and my brother was given a cricket bat. Mum had to organise the change of address for ration books and ID cards and notify various people about our move and the WVS helped with that too. I am sure if it had not been for them, our family and many other bombed out families would have had real problems.

Moreover, the WVS would be called upon to provide such comforts as books and food for the small children of internees, milk for babies and assistance with writing letters to loved ones. When the Local Defence Volunteers were being formed, they had very little equipment. Local resources including the WVS were called upon to assist. Brassards, first aid kits, haversacks and camouflaged sniper suits were among the items made by members some of whom were later engaged on special purpose work, that of making Molotov cocktails for the use of the LDV. But it was the making of tea which became synonymous with the WVS because tea and a listening ear was all that many of those who came into contact with the service expected. Help beyond that was welcome but the extent, to which help was given, surprised everyone.

Christine Lock said
We lived near Totton, but my granddad was with the ARP in Southampton and often during his shifts he would be on the go non-stop especially after a raid. He said that from quite early in the war that as if by magic, the WVS would appear from nowhere and set up a canteen and an information post for those who had been bombed out or who were coming to look for loved ones. He said more than once it was a strong cup of tea and a smile from the ladies of the WVS that lifted his spirits and gave him the energy to carry on.

Mobile canteens and kitchens became the cornerstone of the service provision to troops, Civil Defence workers, those engaged in war work out in the countryside where no suitable facilities were available and to civilians be they evacuees or bombed out families. In fact, anyone on the move in the Forest would have come into contact with a WVS mobile catering facility. They were everywhere and in a short time the organisation had graduated from requisitioned vehicles to its own purpose-built vehicles, a number of which were donated by benefactors from home and overseas.

During this period too, the Housewives Service was enrolling members from villages and communities in the Forest. These volunteers undertook equally valuable tasks including helping with salvage drives, rendering first aid where necessary, helping residents to clear up or salvage belongings, running errands of mercy, providing the use of baths, and sweeping up broken glass from roads and paths. Inevitably, duties included making a 'nice cup of tea'. Within a year of the declaration of war, the WVS had established itself and rightfully so, as the organisation to whom every service man and woman could turn to for help and it would be given to the limits of what was possible. Notwithstanding the demands placed upon the organisation by civilians and changing Government needs, typically the expectations of the service can be summed up by an extract from one WVS area report.

'Tea at one hour's notice for any number of people between forty and four hundred has become commonplace. Baths, laundry, salads, knitting of pullovers and socks to men, altar flowers for chaplains, decorations for the Mess, upholstery of chairs and sofas, provision of furniture on a hire purchase scheme, cakes and sandwiches for Concert Parties, billets for wives and children, constant supervision of the welfare of crews of Anti-Aircraft sites'

It was concluded that whenever there was a job of any kind which was nobody's particular responsibility, it was handed to the women of the WVS, and it was always done.

The incredibly long list of jobs undertaken by the WVS also included changing library books for hospital patients, helping with national savings campaigns including Warships Week and Salute the Soldier, making children's toys from recovered wood, finding furnished rooms, organising salvage drives, helping children's homes every morning and afternoon by taking the youngsters for walks, making blackout blinds, and acting as a Registry for queries on housing, tax, and many other issues. They also located and prepared and cleaned homes for evacuees and others in need, organised basic furniture items end even placed flowers in vases as a welcome gesture. When the United States began sending troops to Britain, the WVS evolved the idea of British Welcome Clubs in which GI's could meet young people of the neighbourhood. Local clubs were often based on or near the airfields and these were to contribute in no small way to acclimatising the population and the incoming Americans, to each other's way of life. And all this was done by volunteers almost all of whom covered all their own expenses.

Robert Read recalls
I was involved in one of the big building contracts in readiness for the Normandy Campaign. These girls used to come out in all weather, to our site on the Beaulieu River, through rain, mud, and very cold weather to serve us with food and drink. Whatever

the day chucked at them they always managed a smile and a few kind words. One time a lass called Jane just accidentally slipped in the mud and went over. I am afraid she showed a bit too much leg on that occasion and although thankfully she was not hurt, her pride was dented. After that we used to call her our Daily Mirror girl after the pin up 'Jane' who appeared in the paper.

One cannot make mention of the WVS without including one rather unique aspect of the Service which, with little recognition from the wider public, made a significant contribution to the war effort. The COGS scheme was to involve local children in the task of the collection of salvage and to make the task more interesting a badge was awarded to the keenest young collectors. The scheme, which had the support of parents and the Educational Authorities, was to award a total of 192,523 badges although it was recognised that many more than that number were earned during the period when the scheme was operational. The children had their own COGS song and 'as little cogs in a big wheel' they made a tangible and much needed contribution, not only to the war effort, but to the breadth of services offered by the Women's Voluntary Service.

Joyce Wilson said
I helped to collect salvage in Totton at weekends and evening after school and I had several friends and we used to go out in a group to collect paper and all sorts of scrap that we could carry and then take to the collection centre near Testwood. I missed out on a badge but often our little group would get sweets from passing soldiers so that made up for it.

Left: Children could volunteer to collect scrap under the WVS COGS scheme . They were awarded badges for good service. (AmiS)
Right: Collecting items for recycling, another job for he WVS

During the war members of the Women's Institute branches in Hampshire also made a significant contribution to supporting those in the Armed Services and Emergency Services and in addition they were active in food production and preservation. An Education and Home Produce Committee organised the canning and bottling of locally grown fruits which were stored in garages, kitchens, and village halls. Some 37 tons of jam was produced across Hampshire as a result. Growing potatoes was another essential activity. WI branches in the New Forest, distributed seed potatoes to members and ran competitions to find out who could grow the most. Local hospitals were the beneficiaries of the annual potato harvest.

In partnership with the WVS, the county Women's Institute helped with the Pie Scheme, also known as the Rural Pie Scheme and the Meat Pie Scheme created by the Ministry of Food. The WVS had been delivering food to Service personnel on remote sites such as Anti-Aircraft and Observer Corps sites throughout the New Forest since the early war years. The scheme expanded to include farm workers and people living in rural communities that were without access to canteens and British Restaurants (Government organised community catering centres). The meat content of the pie was two ounces, from Government stocks, and licensed bakers produced batches according to local demand. The pies were sold without coupons for 4d (2 pence) and only one pie per person was permitted. Milford-on-Sea Women's Institute records show that they were selling 1000 pies per week.

Throughout the dark, traumatic, and eventful days of the Second World War, the post war repatriation of POWS and the homecoming of the nation's service men and women, in the streets, lanes and villages of the New Forest, the Women's Voluntary Service could be found involved in every aspect of daily life, helping everyone without exception, whatever their needs. As with every other woman's wartime service, the women of the WVS in the subsequent rebuilding of Britain and in the resettlement of its population went about their business without fuss or favour and displayed extraordinary courage, selflessness, and determination for the good of all those they served.

Fire Crews constantly trained while on duty
(CCFF)

8

In Case of Fire

Fire cover was provided at all New Forest military camps, fire stations, supply depots, airfields and at other prime locations as the build-up to D-Day began apace.

From late 1943, the country's Fire Force Areas (operational areas) were graded into three categories for the purpose of a new operational plan, known as the Colour Scheme. As part of this, reinforcing personnel, many of whom were women, moved into the south of England, including the New Forest.

Blue Areas were at highest risk, and they were reinforced. These forward areas soon became vast tented cities for Allied troops, and many new airfields were constructed as bases for the USAAF and the RAF. Green Areas were classified as being at moderate risk. In the Brown Areas, personnel and equipment were reduced because of the prolonged absence of enemy attack. This scheme is relatively unknown, and it is therefore worth exploring it in some detail.

An Operational Memorandum was prepared with great care, and detailed guidance was given to Fire Force Commanders in the Blue, Green and Brown Areas to show them how the scheme was to operate. Fire Force 14, for example, was classified as a Blue Area, so the Fire Force Commander was faced with the immediate prospect of an influx of reinforcing personnel of all ranks, both men and women, and a proportionate increase in the number of appliances. Arthur Stevens recalled:

As the war progressed, preparations began for D-Day and there was a lot of activity in our local area. We were being sent fire service reinforcements from London and the Midlands to strengthen our numbers, and we then were given an extra vehicle which was housed in a garage next door to the station. One important job which we did was working with some of the Canadians at Lepe near Beaulieu in the New Forest, on the PLUTO pipeline which was being tested under the Solent, and we had to pump fresh water through, and it would come out at the other end, that is, on the Isle of Wight.

Throughout the early years of the war the nation's fire services had, it was acknowledged, performed work over and above the call of duty in controlling the thousands of fires caused by enemy air raids. As the plans for the invasion of occupied Europe accelerated in the autumn of 1943, it became clear that

A pre-war German Aerial photograph of Christchurch Airfield (AC)

the NFS was to take a key role, particularly in those regions of the country from which any attack on the continent was to be launched. In this advanced stage of the war, the needs of the civilian population, whilst still receiving attention, were to be subordinated in the invasion launch areas in favour of the need to assist the armed forces.

By the time the invasion day dawned, the NFS (National Fire Service) was ready for all emergencies. During the weeks that followed, all calls for assistance were responded to promptly and each man gave of his best.

A similar set of circumstances had occurred during the late summer of 1943 when Exercise Harlequin had been staged. This exercise involved the marshalling and embarkation of troops and equipment from ports on the south coast, and their journey by sea to within a few miles of the French coast. This 'trailing of their coat', as it was called by the Allied Forces, had evoked no response from the enemy other than a minor raid on Portsmouth on the first night of the exercise, when sixty-three fires were attended by the NFS. The build-up of the Armed Services and the reinforcement of target areas by the NFS had been carried out in a realistic manner, and many lessons had been learned. These were to prove of tremendous value in the months to come. Fire Captain Cyril Kendall from Reading recorded:

In 1944, one interesting thing was that on all the main roads down the country there were slabs of concrete on the side of the road. We got an order saying that the company, mine was St George's Company, was to go to a particular point for which we were given a map reference. When we arrived, a despatch rider told us to place our trailer pumps on each of the concrete slabs which were placed every so many hundreds of yards apart, and we were to wait there for two hours. Well, we had only been there for a short time when literally hundreds of army lorries convoyed past us on the way to the south of England. Our job was to protect the men and vehicles from fires that might break out in the vehicles, and in fact we did have fun with a couple of ammunition lorries which exploded. No one was hurt and the convoy was uninterrupted by the fires.

Jill Potter recalls what she saw as an eight-year-old girl:
I saw many fire engines and men in the Forest area for quite some time, and that must have been about the time when all the troops were coming here for what we later knew of course to be in readiness for D-Day. I was told after the war, by the way, that the fire crews were needed to look after the military camps which were being filled up with men and equipment and lorries, and all that sort of thing. If my memory serves me well, I did hear of a lorry full of ammunition blowing up near Southampton, so I suppose that is the sort of thing that the fire brigade had to deal with.

Improvements to reinforcement bases were made following Exercise Harlequin, particularly with the knowledge of military movements and the possible contingencies following damage by enemy action to main transport routes. NFS convoys were not to exceed five appliances, because it was considered that larger formations were less likely to be able to overtake military convoys in an emergency. NFS despatch riders were trained on convoy runs and requested to use non-military routes where necessary.

Certain roads in the Forest were made one-way only by the military authorities to meet the needs of service traffic in embarkation and back areas. This necessitated changes in predetermined attendance arrangements, as stations were frequently rendered much more remote from certain risks because of the roundabout routes that had to be taken. Predetermined attendances also had to be arranged for camps and vehicle parks. In view of the closure of certain roads it was vital that despatch riders should gain knowledge of alternative routes for convoy purposes. The despatch riders who had been transferred under the Colour Scheme also had to become fully acquainted with local topography. Frequent reinforcing exercises were accordingly arranged between neighbouring areas and regions so that personnel could undertake exercises focusing on the routes they should follow and the location of rendezvous points and reinforcement bases.

The fact that members of the NFS lived for months under canvas with the Army in the camps was probably the best demonstration of the liaison that existed between the two services. During Exercise Harlequin, units of the Army Fire Service were moved down to the southern part of the area for the purpose of supplementing existing NFS cover. These units worked in close cooperation with the NFS and were mobilised through the nearest Sub-Divisional Control. Arrangements were made so that Army Fire Service units could be called upon to assist at fires that did not involve military establishments and this practice helped to train the Army in practical firefighting. Many exercises were carried out in the Forest with sections of the Army Fire Service to this end. Training included water relaying over open country or in built-up areas for the purpose of gaining experience in ramping, positioning of pumps and various traffic problems. What were known as pipeline exercises were organised at Hatchett's Pond, near Beaulieu and there were also exercises involving the use of fireboats on Southampton Water. Ronald John Tilling, a former dock worker, wrote:

Positioned right round the docks at Southampton were many fire pumps and probably a couple of hundred men ready to assist if anything happened when we were loading stores, fuel, and vehicles onto the assortment of craft that had tied up here in the weeks prior to 6 June. I know that fireboats based in Southampton Water went out many times to deal with fire problems on some of the ships in the Solent armada.

Air support for the invasion presented its own additional risk to the NFS in Hampshire. In the New Forest, there were densely populated military conurbations during the build-up to D-Day, with camps, stores, depots and permanent and temporary airfields. The airfields were used by many types of British and American aircraft, and these were mainly fighters, including the Typhoon and Hurricane, and fighter-bombers such as the P47 Thunderbolt. However, larger aircraft including the Wellington, Flying Fortress and Halifax, were also flying out of the area.

The numbers of aircraft increased as the clock counted down to 6 June, and so too did the number of sorties from every airfield. This increased aircraft presence brought with it some major challenges for the NFS,

The former Control Tower at Ibsley (AC)

and inevitably many calls during the months of April, May and June 1944 were to aeroplane crashes. In fact, during this period there were fifty-two recorded crashes within the tight-knit network of airfields in south and west Hampshire alone. In contrast, only forty-seven call outs to crashes were recorded in the previous year to December 1943. It must be remembered that many of the airfields were in close proximity to one another and airspace was at a premium and unfortunately on more than one occasion collisions took place.

RAF Ibsley was one of the larger permanent airfields, and there are still signs of wartime occupation although much of the site is now a peaceful nature reserve. It was not always so quiet, however. One summer morning in 1944 a fighter aircraft crashed shortly after take-off from the main north–south concrete runway. Immediately, a call was sent to the local NFS station and simultaneously a call was put out to the USAAF crash tender stationed on the airfield. As the American vehicle arrived on the scene, the bomb payload on the stricken aircraft exploded, setting both the aircraft and the crash tender alight. Fortunately, the pilot escaped the mayhem, but the tender crew lost their lives.

On 29 June in the same year, a P47 Thunderbolt crashed and demolished a bungalow not far from the Christchurch airfield at Somerford, then several hours later the same pilot in another aircraft took off from the same aerodrome and crashed again, this time blowing up the fire appliance which had been on stand-by after the previous incident. The blast from the explosion brought down a second aircraft that had taken off at the same time. The fires and resulting damage caused by exploding bombs killed fourteen people including two civilians, one of whom was a fireman. Among the twenty-two who were injured, two were firemen.

In addition to dealing with aviation-related incidents, the firemen providing cover for the military during the build-up to D-Day also dealt with call outs to heath and gorse fires which threatened ammunition dumps, stores and the 'tented cities' which housed troops. As one fireman commented, 'Travelling through the county we saw what seemed like hundreds of trailer pumps, hundreds of tented camps for the Army and American Thunderbolts flying overhead. What a sight and one I will never forget.'

In Germany, meanwhile, the Führer had on 16 May ordered the long-range V-1 (Vengeance Weapon, Fzg 76) bombardment of England to commence in June. His order stated that 'The bombardment would open like a thunderclap by night.'

Notes from the Fire Force diary capture the situation at the time:

7 June 1944
There had been no enemy action during the previous night although large concentrations of Allied aircraft had continued operations from this country. One interesting feature of the previous evening had been the flight over HQ of hundreds of four-engine bombers, each one towing a large glider at an altitude of about 1000 feet. These gliders are capable of carrying a load of 30 fully armed soldiers. Large convoys of re-enforcements, lorries, tanks, bulldozers, and steamrollers were encountered on the roads.

8 June 1944
500 German prisoners were landed, and selected prisoners were interrogated by Intelligence Officers. An NFS officer who witnessed the landing commented on the arrogant bearing of these prisoners.

After the frenetic activity of the early months of 1944, which culminated in the mass movement of military men and machines out of the Blue Zone from 6 June, the Fire Services then faced the unknown terrors of the flying bombs. But by September the tide was turning, and a more upbeat mood swept the country.

8 September 1944
As decreed by Adolph Hitler, the first V-1 rockets were launched against London. This rocket was only accurate to within a ten-mile radius of the target and was vulnerable to anti-aircraft fire. More than half the rockets fired at England were brought down by the Anti-Aircraft gun batteries along the south coast. Nevertheless, the damage caused

by those rockets which penetrated the AA screen and arrived at the targets, was substantial and casualties exceeded 6000 dead.
[NB. The later variant, the V-2 rocket arrived silently, unlike its noisy predecessor, and over 500 of these reached London, killing a total of 2,724 people.]

Another note, dated 11 September 1944, was entered into the Fire Force Logbook:
The Allied invasion of the Continent has brought many pleasant surprises, not the least of which is the lack of enemy retaliation on the country. Everyone had expected at the outset that there would have been heavy bombing attacks along the south coast and with the arrival of the flying bomb, some serious situations could have developed very easily. As things have gone however, the prospect of enemy air activity is receding fast and the time has come for the personnel who were sent to reinforce this Area in the early part of the year, to return to the North of England.

Many requests were received by the Regional Commissioner's Office from both firemen and firewomen who asked to be allowed to stay in the south. However, only in exceptional cases was permission granted, and those who were accepted had to forfeit all right to lodging allowances, reverting to the same status as those whose homes were in the area.

When repatriation began, most firemen and women were sent in phases from their various fire stations to the Alresford Reinforcement Base, Arlebury Park, near Winchester in Hampshire, from where they either entrained from the local railway station or taken the 10 miles by road to Alton railway station for onward travel to other parts of the country.

The level of cover given by the Colour Scheme was maintained until November 1944, when the progress of the war dictated that it be phased out and personnel returned to their respective forces. Many friendships were forged between fellow firefighters who had come together in a unique set of circumstances to play their part in safeguarding potentially vulnerable parts of the country, as well as providing a fire protection 'insurance policy' for the thousands of men who were encamped throughout the south on the eve of the liberation of occupied Europe. Words alone cannot begin to describe the sometimes arduous, but always purposeful, journey that was undertaken by the nation's Fire Services between 1937 and the final months of the war.

Another view of the former control tower at RAF Ibsley
(Authors Collection)

9

Through Adversity to the Stars

Towards the end of the First World War, General Jan Smuts, the distinguished South African-born soldier, was the chair of a committee which was tasked with looking at measures for Britain's Home Defence, for it was clear that much had been learnt during the previous years of conflict about the nation's capabilities and inabilities.

It was Smuts who was quoted as saying that 'The day might not be far off when aerial operations may become the principal operations of war, to which the older forms of military operations may become secondary and subordinate.' He went on to recommend that the existing Royal Flying Corps (RFC) should be amalgamated with the Royal Naval Air Squadron, and this became a reality in April 1918. The RAF was formed just seven months before the 11 November 1918 Armistice, at which time it was the largest air service in the world with more than 22,000 aircraft at its disposal, many of which were built in Hampshire.

East Boldre Airfield in the New Forest, which opened in 1910 for pleasure flying, was closed just a year, or so later and then reopened in 1915 as Flying Training School, RFC Beaulieu. Expansion of the site in 1917 included an additional three hangars as well as workshops and barracks.

RFC Beaulieu hosted 16 Training Squadron, flying Avro 504s, B.E.2cs and Curtiss Jennys, and this squadron arrived in December 1916. In November 1917, 59 Squadron, which flew Sopwith Camels, arrived; 79 Squadron with Sopwith Dolphins arrived in August 1917, leaving in February 1918; 84 Squadron was formed in January 1917 with B.E.2cs and B.E.12as, departing in March of the same year; 103 Squadron with various types of plane formed in September 1917 and left the same month; 117 Squadron with DH.4s and R.E.8s was formed in January 1918 and disbanded in July 1918; and finally 29 Training Depot Station was formed in July 1918 from 59 Squadron and 79 Squadron.

During the summer of 1919, Hugh Trenchard worked on the challenging task of completing the RAF's demobilisation and establishing it on a peace-time basis. There was a huge post-war budget earmarked for the demolition of existing airfield infrastructures at the end of hostilities, and it was proposed that the RAF would dramatically reduce in size, from 188 squadrons to around twenty-five. Beaulieu was one of many stations that were no longer needed as the RAF reorganised for its new operational conditions, and it was abandoned just a few months after the end of the war, in 1919. Worth noting, however, is that nearby Calshot, on the spit at the end of Southampton Water close to Lepe, in use as a flying boat base from 1913, remained operational. It was officially commissioned in February 1922 as RAF Calshot.

It was also during this time that the new RAF officer ranks were decided upon, despite some opposition from members of the Army Council. Trenchard was regraded from Major General to Air Vice Marshal, then promoted to Air Marshal a few days later.

By the autumn of 1919, the effects of Lloyd George's 'Ten Year Rule' were causing Trenchard some difficulty as he sought to develop the institutions of the Royal Air Force. Simply put, the Ten-Year Rule was based on a premise that a war-weary world would not engage in any further conflict for a least a decade. So, Trenchard had to argue against the view that the Army and Royal Navy should provide support services and education, leaving the RAF to focus only on flying training. He viewed this idea as a precursor to the break-up of the RAF, and yet despite the cost he wanted his own institutions, which would develop airmanship and engender the spirit of the air. Although Trenchard attained a measure of financial security, the future of the RAF was far from assured. He judged that the chief threat to his position came from the new First Sea Lord, Admiral Beatty. And so, seeking to take the initiative, Trenchard arranged to meet him. Arguing that the 'air is one and indivisible', Trenchard put forward a case for an air force with its own strategic role, which would also control army and navy cooperation squadrons. Perhaps not surprisingly, Beatty did not accept this argument, so Hugh Trenchard resorted to asking for a twelve-month amnesty before changes were made. This request appealed to Beatty's

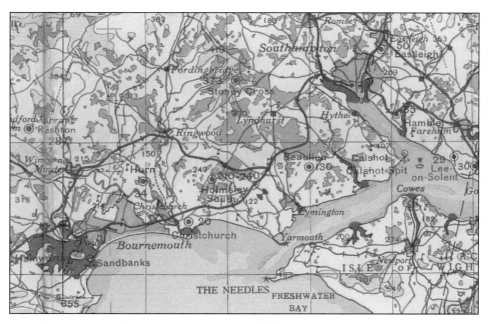

A mid war RAF map showing the permanent airfields at Hurn, Beaulieu. Stoney Cross, Christchurch and Holmsley South (Authors Collection)

sense of fair play, and he agreed to it, giving Trenchard until the end of 1920 to produce detailed plans. It was around this time that Trenchard indicated to Beatty that control over some supporting elements of naval aviation might be returned to the Admiralty. Trenchard also offered Beatty the option of locating Air Ministry staff who worked with naval aviation at the Admiralty. Beatty declined the offer and later, when no transfer of any naval aviation assets occurred, came to the view that Trenchard had acted in bad faith.

Having convinced Churchill of his case, Trenchard oversaw the founding of the RAF (Cadet) College at Cranwell as the world's first military air academy. Later, in 1920, he inaugurated the Aircraft Apprentice scheme, which provided the RAF with specialist ground crew. He also sought to secure the future of the RAF by finding an active fighting role for the new service, and in 1920 he successfully argued that the service should take the lead during operations to restore peace in Somaliland. The success of this small air action allowed Trenchard to put the case for the RAF's policing of the Empire. Controversially, earlier the same year he had written that the RAF could even suppress industrial disturbances or uprisings in mainland Britain.

The idea was not to Churchill's liking, and he instructed Trenchard not to refer to this proposal again.

During the early 1920s, the continued independent existence of the RAF and its control of naval aviation were subject to a series of governmental reviews. The Balfour report of 1921, the Geddes Axe of 1922 and the Salisbury Committee of 1923 all found in favour of the RAF, despite lobbying from the Admiralty and opposition in Parliament. On every occasion, Hugh Trenchard and his staff officers worked to prove that the RAF provided good value for money and was required for the long-term strategic security of the United Kingdom.

Some correspondents at the time referred to a poem (it is displayed at RAF Cranwell), apparently written in 1797, as the inspiration behind those who were for the maintenance and enhancement of an effective air defence.

The time will come when thou shalt lift thine eyes.
To watch a long-drawn battle in the skies
While aged peasants too amazed for words
Stare at the flying fleets of wondrous birds
England so long the mistress of the sea
Where winds and waves confess her sovereignty
Her ancient triumph yet on high shall bear.
And reign, the sovereign of the conquered air.

In 1922 the RAF was given control of all British Forces in Iraq. The RAF also carried out Imperial air policing over India's North-West Frontier province. In the same year, the RAF Staff College at Andover, Hampshire, was set up to provide RAF-specific training for middle-ranking officers. Yet the RAF still only had twelve squadrons on airfields across the country, very unlike the situation in France – which possessed the best-equipped air force in Europe.

The story of the fledgling years of the RAF is not too dissimilar to its story in the twenty-first century, for it includes unworkable ideas, political careers, budget cuts and indecision, underlined by improvements in some areas. Under Stanley Baldwin's government of 1923–4, agreement was reached on the creation of a Home Defence Air Force and the provision of mobile and fixed sound locators (an early radar system). Later, and still under Baldwin, who returned to power from late 1924, new bomber stations were grouped geographically: the areas included Hampshire. Less than two decades later the New Forest was to accommodate a network of air-fields, or air stations as they were also called, in addition to the existing flying boat station at Calshot and a site at Christchurch, all of which played a vital role in the preparations for and launch of D-Day in 1944.

The Ten-Year Rule was abolished in 1932, coinciding with an acknowledgement that the RAF was in a position of weakness with only a few aircraft, some of which were obsolete. New permanent aerodrome building began under a scheme, com-monly known as the Expansion Programme, in 1934, in recognition of the long overdue need for 'permanent' bases for the RAF, which was to increase in strength in a phased manner over the coming years. In seeking to match the strength of Ger-many's Luftwaffe, the British Government introduced schemes for the expansion of the Royal Air Force. These schemes quickly followed one after the other during the five years 1934 to 1939. The Cabinet passed just five schemes, these were known as A, C, F, L, M which resulted in a major construction programme, providing for the modernisation of existing RAF stations bringing them up to standard with the new aerodromes being built during the years 1934 to 1940.

These new aerodromes were built to a standard design with variations to suit local conditions. Each site included most of the same technical buildings, including water tower, control tower, station headquarters, parachute store, workshops, central

Left: One of the early post war military buildings which stood on the site of the WW2 Radar Station at Sopley. Now a housing estate (Authors Collection.)
Right: One of the surviving air raid shelters at former RAF Beaulieu (Marc Heighway)

heating station, bomb and ammunition stores, motor transport pool and operations block, engine house, guardroom, fire engine garage, fuel store and gunnery range. In addition, there were offices, locker rooms, wireless rooms and aircraft equipment stores, hangars, accommodation, canteens, wash rooms and rest rooms.

The Air Ministry Directorate General of Works (AMDGW) was responsible for organising the largest constructional programme in Britain's history. In late 1945 a periodical called The Aeroplane contained an article which stated that in process of creating the temporary airfields, the country became 'one vast aircraft carrier anchored off the north-west coast of Europe'. Indeed, there were 720 operational airfields at wars end.

The Forests contribution is listed below. In the airfield summaries, please note that the following abbreviations are used: NVR (no visible remains); SVR (some visible remains). Both designations are correct at time of print however it's worth noting that whilst further evidence of war in the Forest is being discovered every year, existing sites may change appearance or ownership so please make sure you research each site for up-to-date information.

Christchurch
Pundit code XC (the identity code of the airfield: a beacon was set to flash the relevant letter or letters to confirm the name of the aerodrome to aircraft overhead). Already established at the outbreak of the Second World War, the aerodrome had an interesting history spanning the previous two decades. On the boundary of the New Forest, Christchurch was in Hampshire at the time; now it is in Dorset because of boundary changes. The runways included grass, concrete and steel matting, a total of five in all. There were five hangars, including three 'blister' types in preparation for war service. It acted as a satellite for nearby Hurn and Ibsley airfields under No. 10 Group, Fighter Command. It became operational in 1940.
(NVR)

Ibsley
Pundit code IB, call sign LARDIT. This airfield was built by various contractors and opened in early 1941, with three tarmac runway sites and twelve hangars. Many variants of the Spitfire and the Hurricane Mk I flew from Ibsley. Based here were 32, 66, 118, 129, 165, 234, 263, 302, 310, 312, 313, 421, 453, 501, 504 and 616 Squadrons.

It transferred between the RAF and the USAAF on two occasions.
(SVR, in private ownership)

Beaulieu
Pundit code BU, call sign ARCHEBACK. Beaulieu Heath was on the opposite side of
the road to the First World War East Boldre airfield and was opened in the autumn
of 1942 having been built by various contractors to the standard three runway design.
To begin with it had two T2 hangars and a single blister type, and it was variously
home to 257, 263 and 486 Squadrons flying Typhoons and Tempests. In the early
days, most personnel had tented accommodation, and the operations room and
control tower were of temporary construction. No. 224 Squadron, flying Liberator
111As, arrived in September to bolster the U-boat offensive in the Bay of Biscay.
Halifax's of 405 and 158 Squadrons, Royal Canadian Air Force, arrived to take part
in strikes against enemy shipping. Later in the war, in the post D-Day period, various
aircraft including B26 Marauders flew into this airfield on the way to France. Lysanders carrying SOE agents also flew from Beaulieu, the nearby village being home to
various training establishments. Beaulieu Airfield was put under the control of the
USAAF in May 1944 and reverted to RAF control in September of the same year.
(SVR)

Holmsley South
Pundit code HM; call sign RECESS.
This airfield was built by John Laing
and Son Ltd and opened under
Coastal Command in September
1942. With three runways and five
T2 hangars it was a large aerodrome,
flying Spitfires, Typhoons and Mus-
tangs. It passed to the USAAF in
June 1944 and then to RAF Trans-
port Command in October 1944.
(SVR)

*418 Squadron RCAF Mosquito was based at
Holmsley South*

Hurn
Pundit code KU. This was also a large aerodrome, boasting three concrete runways
and seventeen hangars including four T2 types. It hosted Typhoons and Mosqui-

toes from 125, 164, 181, 182, 183, 193, 197, 198, 247, 257, 263 and 266 Squadrons. Opened in the summer of 1941. Forty pilots based at RAF Hurn were invited to a party to meet families in the neighbourhood and visit their homes. It was a great success, witnessed by British and American Welfare Officers and the pilots were very loud in their appreciation of their hosts. Subsequently, a list of local families who would welcome enlisted men was given to the authorities and new friendships were forged and maintained, in some cases, long after D-Day. Hurn is now known as Bournemouth Airport which is operated by Regional & City Airports (RCA). (SVR)

Needs Oar Point
Pundit code NI. This 'field was opened in April 1944, for D-Day only, right on the coast at St Leonard's in the New Forest. The site had two runways of steel matting and four Blister hangars. It flew Typhoons from 193 and 197 Squadrons. Domestic accommodation was in tents, and the nearby farmhouse at Park Farm was used for units including Intelligence and Radio.
(SVR, in private ownership)

Stoney Cross
Pundit code SS. Call sign IRONWORK. Situated in the north of the Forest, Stoney Cross was opened in November 1942, although at that time it was still under construction by George Wimpey and Co. Ltd. With a typical three concrete runway layout, this site was originally conceived to serve as a 'secret' airfield, deliberately devoid of any of the usual facilities and with camouflaged hides for aircraft, although the exact reason it was to be secret remains open to conjecture. It was subsequently designated as an advance base for both fighters and bombers, and in the process, it expanded from about 500 to 900 acres, yet its construction was delayed because of disagreements over how much compensation was to be paid to commoners who grazed their cattle on the site. An

A Lidar image taken above Stoney Cross (NFNPA)

agreement was eventually reached, and the six-month delay in starting work was overlooked by the authorities. The agreement to pay compensation at the rate of 2s 6d per acre was subsequently cancelled under a War Requisitions Act.

Discovering the remains of a runway light at Stoney Cross (M.Knott)

Four new generation T2 hangars were erected, as were six blister types. Flying Hurricanes, Ventura's, Stirling's, and the widely criticised Albemarle's from 175, 297 and 299 Squadrons were based here. Stoney Cross was operated by the RAF and later the USAAF (Station 452) flying Mitchells.

There are several features at the south-eastern end of the airfield immediately adjacent to the main A31 that may represent features of an anti-aircraft site. These include a possible searchlight emplacement, a gun-laying radar position, a radio mast, and foxholes. These features are not recorded on the RAF maps of the airfield, but further investigation may be able to identify them more positively.

An ancillary site of Stoney Cross airfield, the sick quarters at Castle Malwood/ Stoney Cross, was built to accommodate ill and injured staff. Such facilities were a necessary feature of any military structure, and consisted of wards, a mortuary, an ambulance garage, and nursing staff quarters. The RAF site plan refers to an HF (high frequency) transmitting station located immediately east of this sick quarters area.

Stoney Cross airfield was released by the War Ministry in 1948 and largely demolished a few years later. As with many sites around the New Forest, it is possible that this demolition was only surface deep, leaving many platforms and foundations intact. The site of the sick quarters presently lies alongside the A31, which will almost certainly have disrupted the site when it was made into a dual carriageway in the 1960s. The HF station may conceivably have been a particularly tall structure, therefore leaving deep foundations.
(SVR)

Incidentally, depending on which reference source is used, the cost of a typical heavy bomber station in 1941 was, without services and buildings, estimated at £500.000 with the cost for a fully operational site quoted as between £850.000 and £1.000.000.

Winkton

Pundit code XT, call sign DRAINSINK. This was an advanced landing ground for D-Day only, with two steel matting runways and four blister-type hangars. It was used by the USAAF under the control of 11 Group, RAF Fighter Command. Opened in March 1944, it was closed less than a year later.
(SVR, in private ownership)

Calshot

Call sign STAMMER. Situated on the spit at the end of Southampton Water, Calshot entered the war for flying boat training, using the Singapore and Stranraer biplane flying boats of 201, 209 and 240 Squadrons. It was a service centre for Sunderland's and an operational base for Air Sea Rescue launches. The original flying boat sheds and some original buildings remain in use to this day. One of the most intriguing aspects of Calshot's wartime history is its use as a base for Heinkel HE 115 Floatplanes. A number of these enemy planes were flown to England by Norwegian pilots and at least one was subsequently pressed into service by British Intelligence. We know that one of the Heinkel's completed thirty-eight missions into enemy territory. We also know that the two floats on the plane were fitted with electric motors so that when the main engines were cut, the plane could manoeuvre quietly through the water. The floats were hollowed out and fitted with seats and a small protective glass shield. An agent would sit in each one, making it easier to transfer to a boat or the shore.
(SVR)

Sway

This almost forgotten but vital emergency landing ground (ELG) was used sporadically for just a few months in 1944 and, according to locals, offered no facilities except a grass strip and a guard hut. Aircraft were moved here from time to time from Christchurch, until the enemy bombed Sway in a light attack.
(NVR, in private ownership)

Bisterne

This site was surveyed in 1943 and was deemed suitable for service as an ALG, for use solely as part of the D-Day campaign. Opened in September 1943, basic facilities comprised two steel mesh air strips, hard standings, and an aircraft marshalling area. Four blister hangars were erected, providing better cover for aircraft than the tents provided for the crews. Flying the P-47s of 371st Fighter Group, USAAF, from April 1944, it was not long before the mesh tracking became rutted, and the site had to be temporarily closed for reconstruction. The Thunderbolts moved to Ibsley, before returning on 1 May 1944. The 371st continued its assaults on occupied Europe. Post D-Day the site was soon abandoned, and it was derelict by July 1944. (NVR, in private ownership)

Pylewell, also known as Lymington.

This ALG was created on the Pylewell Estate, which was already being used by other armed services units. Great swathes of woodland were removed to lay steel mesh for two temporary runways on Snooks Farm and several blister hangars were erected. The 9th Tactical Air Command of the USAAF arrived in March 1944 with P47 Thunderbolts, and domestic accommodation was mainly under canvas. The site was effectively stood down in July 1944 and returned to farmland. For the most part, all new permanent aerodromes built after the outbreak of war used the dispersal principle of siting various key buildings at a distance from the main runway and hangar complex, as a safety measure in case of concentrated bombing by an enemy. For example, the barns at the junction of Shotts Lane and Lisle Court Road, East End, near Lymington, were used as debriefing rooms.
(NVR of the airfield. Estate in private ownership)

RAF Sopley

A ground control intercept (GCI) radar station was established at Sopley near Bransgore (on land requisitioned from the Manners Estate) in December 1940. The first installation was a mobile unit designed to be set up in just twelve hours and capable of operating all day every day. It was designed to identify enemy bombers and guide home searchlights and night fighter interceptors towards them. RAF Sopley served the night fighter squadrons based at RAF Middle Wallop (near Andover, Hampshire) and nearby RAF Hurn throughout the war. The antenna arrangement used here was so successful that its style was used at several other GCI stations, and Sopley achieved one of the highest success rates of intercepts of any GCI station in the war. In 1941 the installation was upgraded to an 'intermediate transportable' type, and in 1943 Sopley was made into a permanent station with a fixed antenna. Construction took place in an adjacent field and consisted of large brick buildings for operations rooms and equipment with a permanent Type 7 radar antenna alongside. (NVR) The site is now a housing estate.

In 1940, Lord Beaverbrook, Minister of Aircraft Production, began promoting the suggestion that the public, as well as companies and clubs, could pay for aircraft under the banner of contributing to the war effort. But where to start was the question. A price structure was created which set the price of a single-engined fighter such as the Spitfire, at £5,000, a twin-engine machine at £20,000 and a four-engine aeroplane at £40,000. These sums did not reflect the true cost of each but were set at a level that was considered would be attractive to and achievable by fundraisers. For example, the actual cost of a Spitfire in 1940, was £9,850, give or take a few pounds, and it was this aircraft that was the most popular with the public. About 1,000 Presentation Spitfires were donated between 1940 and 1942, representing 11 per cent of the type's total production during the period. Whilst a donation of one or perhaps two aircraft was usual, a whole squadron comprising forty-three Spitfires was donated by Queen Wilhelmina of the Netherlands. Betty Wait, who was posted to Bournemouth during the war, remembers the details of this donation, which was not widely known until the end of the war Word got around in the WAAF's canteen, and a loud cheer went up one evening at dinner. 'We thought that this was a good omen for Great Britain and a real boost to our boys in blue,' she said.

The Buy a Spitfire Fund was a nationwide appeal, with Hampshire's effort being launched by the Mayor of Winchester. There was also a call made to farmers for the 'Hampshire Agricultural Fighter Plane'. Brockenhurst, in the New Forest, excelled by raising many thousands of pounds during various Fund weeks, and the community helped towards the cost of 'The New Forest Spitfire', which became a reality within a year of the appeal's launch. Various newspapers competed to raise more money than their rivals, and the local media, including the Daily Echo from Southampton, did their bit to champion the cause. Tom Amis sold vegetables at the roadside outside his parents' home in Dibden. 'I collected about four shillings, which I was really pleased about. The thought that something I did helped to buy a Spitfire made me proud in a funny sort of way, and when I saw dogfights, I often wondered if any of the planes was one, I helped to buy.'

Apart from helping the war effort, the fundraisers got to see their assigned name painted on the fuselage of the aircraft, close to the cockpit. The aircraft, the men who flew them, those that maintained them, the women of the Women's Royal Air Force and all those involved in operational duties on the Forest airfields, just like their counterparts throughout the country, are remembered for going 'Through adversity to the stars', 'Per ardua ad astra'.

The New Forest Airfields Memorial erected by Friends of the New Forest Airfields of which the Author was an original member (Marc Heighway)

Evacuees enjoy the countryside of the Forest
(Nick Halling)

10

On the Home Front Line

In 1939, at the request of Walter Elliot, Minister of Health, local authorities were preparing to make a survey of available housing accommodation as part of the plan for 'transferring' children and others in an emergency to the homes of those who were willing to take care of them.

At the time the New Forest was considered a haven for evacuees from local towns, such as Southampton, as well as those from farther afield, in the Midlands and the north of England. This was despite the highly visible war construction programme that was under way throughout the area.

The evacuees were at the forefront of an 'invasion of strangers', as one local resident called it in a letter to a local newspaper, and although many youngsters returned home during the period of the 'phoney war', the population of the Forest continued to increase month on month. Some evacuee children returned when the Blitz began, but their numbers were small compared to the large-scale influx of personnel from the armed services, Civil Defence, the Home Guard, and the Women's Land Army (WLA). A commentator at the time wrote:

There I saw girls from the cities, mostly from London, girls who had been shorthand typists, clerks, and shop assistants, learning how to milk and do dairy farming, how to work in the fields and so on. They were a healthy and happy bunch of girls. And those girls were in the advance guard of what can reasonably be called a Land Army.

Noreen Cooper was in the WLA, and her list of 'jobs to be done' makes exhausting reading:

Apart from milking and mucking out, the girls were expected to plant and pick-up potatoes, look after the mangolds [root vegetables mainly used as cattle food] and sugar beet harvests, hay making, rick making, stoking, threshing, and bagging wheat, pea picking, carrot harvesting and bagging, sprout picking, kale cutting, dung spreading and drawing straw for thatching. We were also responsible for fruit picking, feeding the cows, loading, and unloading full and empty milk churns, thistle cutting, dock pulling, rat catching, harnessing, and working with horses, shepherding sheep, and whitewashing the milk sheds. Oh, and keeping out of the way of lecherous farmers.

Well, we had to get the milking done and then we sat on the fence and watched the convoys passing. We were waving, high spirited and we shouted out 'Good Luck' to the men. It was an exciting but nevertheless strange time really. Many of those poor chaps of course would be killed before the eventual end of the war, but for that moment in time there was so much exuberance and good feeling, almost euphoria after the long slog of the previous years of war, and now we knew the end could well be in sight.

Not all land acquisition took place for military purposes. In 1941, the War Agricultural Committee drew up plans to reseed large areas of grazing land to improve the quality of the grass. Although not particularly successful, this was followed by the decision to cultivate large areas of open grazing land in 1944, so that crops and vegetables could be grown.

Away from the farms, at various sites around the New Forest, groups of girls worked alongside men in forest management tasks such as brush burning, sawing, and measuring. The famous American photojournalist turned war correspondent Lee Miller recorded in her 1943 article 'Children of the New Forest' that 'They are the girls of the Timber Corps. Most of them are in their teens or twenties, many of them have taken a degree at University, fifty percent brain, fifty percent brawn, plus plenty of initiative, is the formula for a good forester.' Twenty-nine million cubic feet of timber was earmarked for felling at the outbreak of war, both in the Crown Estates and other forests, with the New Forest being a key source of supply. The Corps helped to clear the undergrowth in these woods, and then trimmed the trees that were felled by the lumberjacks. The girls learnt general forestry skills, sawmill management and tractor driving, and opportunities existed (much more so in the Timber Corps than in the WLA) for roles of greater responsibility, such as supervisor.

As mentioned elsewhere in this book, Holmsley Mill on the A35 between Lyndhurst and Christchurch was one of the central hubs for the Timber Corps in the New Forest during the Second World War, and it is still a working mill. The nearby railway station (the station house is now a restaurant) was the drop off and collection point not just for WLA and Timber Corps members, but also for service personnel stationed at Holmsley South Airfield.

Members of the Timber Corps assisted by local foresters (AimS)

Incidentally, fraternisation between servicemen and women in uniform was discouraged, but as Mary Weller recalled:

One night at our lodgings in Burley, we heard noises outside. Three of us marched outside straight into a few chaps from the local airfield. They were embarrassed at being caught out, but they just hoped to 'catch sight of some pretty girls' and maybe go to the cinema one evening. It was all very clumsy, but very innocent. These men were too afraid to knock on the door and ask us out, instead they hung around outside, but they were too noisy and did not bargain on three strong and confident lassies taking charge of the situation. Did we go to the cinema after all that? Sadly, the men were posted a day or two later, never to be seen again. Life at the time was just so many twists and turns, but we were all in the great struggle together and we had to learn to deal with it.

The Forest as it is today has been shaped by the wartime felling of trees and post war replanting, as well as by the heavy footprint of the massive wartime construction programme. Mary Weller was just one of thousands of women who were called into service and posted to the New Forest; part of a national sisterhood of fifteen million who were conscripted into war production, the armed services, other support services and voluntary work. The government was freely given powers under the National Service (No. 2) Act December 1941 to conscript suitable classes of women for the Forces and through the Registration for Employment Order, to direct women to any civilian employment in which they might be needed. In October 1939, the number of women on the register of unemployed increased by nearly 200,000, at a time when unemployment amongst men was falling. This was in part because many women were engaged in voluntary work and were therefore not registered for employment.

Dorothy Sayer, originally of Walkford, was a volunteer hospital visitor and later served as an Auxiliary Territorial Service despatch rider.
'There was no grumbling or resentment about being called up, we all wanted to do our bit, but there was certainly a lot of grumbling and discontent from impatience and over-enthusiasm to get started in our wartime roles.'

One newspaper commented:
A woman who has made up her mind, following an appeal to her emotions, that she will present herself for national service, leave home, go wherever she is sent and do whatever is required of her, all at some self-sacrifice, feels irritated and frustrated when she is told by some harassed official that she is not wanted at this time.

The use by the military of the Forest and its natural environment as a training area was significantly underpinned by many requisitioned properties and the massive construction programme. In the west of the Forest, Fordingbridge was designated by the military as number 4 Div. Anti-Tank Island and was heavily fortified with thirty anti-tank barriers to which were added roadblocks and trenches. A mined bridge was ready to be demolished if it was in imminent danger of being captured. The anti-tank island was part of both the General Headquarters (GHQ) line and the Southern Command, Ring-

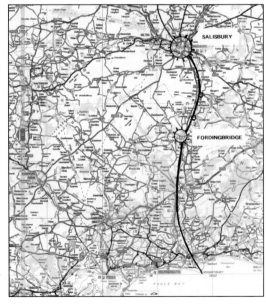

The Avon Valley Stop line through the west of the Forest. (Nigel Walker)

wood Stop Line, mentioned elsewhere in this book, which followed the River Avon from Christchurch to Salisbury via Ringwood. The Stop Line was a line of defences along main roads, rail routes and waterways, built in various parts of Britain to hinder enemy advances in case of a German invasion.

On 14 May 1940, the war effort changed gear when the joy of an early evening radio broadcast of popular music was interrupted by an appeal by the Secretary of State for War in the new Government of Winston Churchill. In preparing for his broadcast, The Rt Hon. Anthony Eden, MP had of course been fully briefed about the sudden and effective German onslaught on Holland, Belgium, Luxembourg, and France, which had taken place in the preceding days. After he had spoken about a possible enemy strike against the country by paratroopers, he raised his listeners' hope by saying that plans for repelling this strike were in place, although he could not spell out exactly what they were. Then, in a clear, resolute voice, the Secretary of State concluded his appeal:

Now is your opportunity. We want large numbers of such men in Great Britain who are British subjects, between the ages of seventeen and sixty-five, to come forward now and offer their service to make assurance doubly sure. The name of the new force, which is now to be raised, will be the Local Defence Volunteers. This name, Local Defence Volunteers, describes its duties in three words. It must be understood that this is, so to speak, a spare-time job, so there will be no need for any volunteer to abandon his present occupation. Part-time members of existing civil defence organisations should ask their officers' advice before registering under the scheme. Men who will ultimately

Ready to defend to the last man, members of a Home Guard unit

become due for calling up under the National Service Act may join temporarily and will be released to join the army when they are required to serve.

Now, a word to those who propose to volunteer. When on duty you will form part of the armed forces, and your period of service will be for the duration of the war. You will not be paid, but you will receive uniform and will be armed. You will be entrusted with certain vital duties, for which reasonable fitness and knowledge of firearms are necessary. These duties will not require you to live away from your homes. To volunteer, what you must do is to give in your name at your local police station and then, as, and when we want you, we will let you know.

This appeal was directed chiefly to those who lived in small towns, villages, and less densely inhabited suburban areas. It was no surprise that Hampshire and the New Forest qualified for the formation of many units. Here was an opportunity for which so many had been waiting, to freely give their help and to keep the country safe.

Whilst many veterans of the First World War, such as Ted Pickles of Totton, were sensitive to 'general talk' of another war, they had quietly been expecting that there would be more conflict in their lifetime. Ted wrote: 'So it was with a heavy heart, true patriotism and a "do or die" resignation that we were to find ourselves once again on the "front line" albeit the front line in our own communities.'

Joy Carter, who lived near Cadnam, recalls her father saying: 'It was expected that we old 'uns would be asked to serve again. If these warmongers had been in the trenches with us first time round, we would never have had another war. I pray for all of you, my dear family.'

Those who were employed on the land had access to a gun of some sort, and if not a gun, then certainly sharp and dangerous farming tools that could be used as weapons. There was a national shortage of weapons as all efforts were being directed to supplying the Armed Services, so an appeal for arms was duly required. From every cupboard, loft, cellar, and secret hideaway came rifles, muskets, and all manner of arms, many of dubious origin and many more of dubious capability. Whilst some units experienced a shortage of all the necessary items, and a newspaper quipped, 'They've got their toothbrushes, the important kit arrives next year,' initiative, improvisation and a steady flow of rifles, helmets and armbands boosted the morale of the men and of those they sought to protect.

Within days of Anthony Eden's appeal, the legal status of the LDV had been established. Detailed instructions about the organisation had been issued and some small groups of volunteers had already taken it upon themselves to patrol their neighbourhoods. By late May 1940, orders were placed in Canada

Home Guard 4th Battalion HG Bournemouth (Hampshire History)

for about 200,000 First World War and later pattern rifles, and these gradually filtered through to the men of the LDV in early July. 'Making do' remained at the core of the LDV's operations, and when the first rifles arrived, they were distributed as best as possible however, many volunteers remained ineffective soldiers because of the lack of basic equipment. Demand by now ad exceeded supply because the number of volunteers had grown to three-quarters of a million.

In mid-July Churchill made a statement in which he referred to the LDV as the 'Home Guard'. With that single comment, he raised the status of the volunteer organisation, further boosted members' morale, and gave them the status they had so far lacked in the eyes of the public. When Lieutenant Colonel Thomas Moore wrote the foreword to the *Home Guard Manual 1941* in July 1940, he said: 'I am glad that the Prime Minister has indicated his desire that our name should be changed.'

Chris Lewis lived near New Milton and recalled that,
*My father was in the local Home Guard, and I often went with them as they patrolled the local area presumably looking for enemy paratroopers or shot-down aircrew. I cannot remember them ever finding anything other than vast amounts of the metallic chaff known as 'window' that was dropped by aircraft to confuse ground radar. For some unknown reason, our larder contained lots of this chaff still in thick wads that had not broken up in the air as it was supposed to. I cannot imagine what my father intended to do with it, but he did tend to hoard things that might come in useful one day. I know that we had bombs dropped in the general area, but I think that death or injury from dropping lumps of chaff would have been more likely here.'

Tom Watson in Bournemouth saw the Home Guard in action, particularly when firing at low flying enemy 'planes.

They stood in place without flinching and shot off round after round at the Messerschmitt's which were flying low and appeared to be firing at everything in sight.

Brian Taylor of Hythe said,

In the early days before they became the Home Guard, they were the butt of many jokes' 'Everyone knows the nickname, look, duck, and vanish. A joke I remember was, How, do you frighten a Home Guard Sentry? Tell him he's a real soldier. But many of the jokes were very rude. I won't repeat what was said. But we needed humour of one sort or another to help relieve the anxiety'.

'I remember my mother being told that in the event of an invasion by the Germans, and remember, there were a lot of scares about invasion in the early days then our house might be used by a gun battery or as a fortification. It was a really old and very sturdy farmhouse set in the trees, so it was to some degree I suppose, well camouflaged.

Bill Chivers said,

In Fordingbridge, there were regular guard duties on the Avon River bridge, the Avon was on a GHQ stop line and along its length were defensive positions, both hidden and in plain sight. Some of the Home Guard personnel had ponies and horses for which it is understood they were giving a small allowance when they used them for patrols. Italian POWs helped with hauling timber cut from the Forest by the Timber Corps and most prisoners were friendly and glad to be out of the war. They made gifts for some of the Home Guard including cigarette lights from spent bullets.

Membership of the volunteer organisation soon exceeded a million men, and one unit had made the first Home Guard kill, shooting down an enemy aircraft with nothing more than rifle fire. The issue of full battledress was approved. Some units were issued with light machine guns, and as the year progressed 'making do' was replaced by 'making up' for lost time, and by improvement, heralded no doubt by the establishment of a dedicated Home Guard training centre.

The *Home Guard Manual 1941* was described in the foreword as 'a little book', although it ran to over 200 pages and was not something you could carry in the top pocket of a battledress blouse. Nonetheless it was a comprehensive, revamped version of the standard manual that had originally been issued to the Regular Army during the First World War, the giveaway being the sketches of soldiers wearing puttees.

Breamore, near Fordingbridge, had a contingent of mounted Home Guardsmen, their horses being stabled at Breamore House. The duties of these men included riding across the Forest looking for enemy parachutists.

Mounted Home Guard in the vicinity of Ringwood and Breamore (Breamore Estate)

On Waterside, (the communities that stretch from Totton to Calshot in Hampshire), Police Constable Kemp, who was based at Hythe police station, worked closely with the local Home Guard detachment. He wrote:

Many of the men were veterans of the Great War, they may have seemed too old, but in fact they were ready to die for their country and they knew a trick or two to throw an enemy off balance. Because we overlook Southampton, this area was on high alert and the chaps were always out training somewhere or other in the Forest, especially on the weapons ranges at Matley Plain.

It was not until 1943 that Noel Coward highlighted the plight of the volunteer soldiers in a song that had some home truths embedded in its whimsical lyrics. Examples of the verses include, 'Could you please oblige us with a Bren gun, or failing that, a hand grenade will do, we've got some ammunition, in a rather damp condition, And Major Huss has an arquebus that was used at Waterloo.' (An arquebus was an early muzzle-loaded firearm used between the fifteenth and seventeenth centuries.)

The Home Guard served their local villages and towns very well and as time passed, they were held in greater esteem. These selfless volunteers, despite all the jibes in the early years, proved to be a determined and reputable defence force.

An Auxiliary Patrol photographed somewhere in Hampshire (C.A.R.T.)

11

Patrolling in the Shadows

The Home Guard was the visible presence of local defence, and they were to become highly regarded morale boosters for the public. However, the debate continues to this day about its potential capabilities as a fighting force against an experienced enemy.

There is no doubt that the Home Guard would have made its presence felt, during any defensive challenges that it may experience. Yet there was a lesser known, but potentially more potent defence organisation in existence. Indeed, its very existence was on a need-to-know basis, and few needed to know, this included family members. Britain's 'secret army', also known as Churchill's secret army and Churchill's guerrilla army, comprised some 4,000 men and some women (unofficially), all courageous volunteers who were prepared from the outset to sacrifice their lives if a German invasion of Britain took place. Formed into units or cells across the country and issued with top secret orders, if church bells rang to warn of enemy invasion the Auxiliary Unit (AU) volunteers were to disappear without telling anyone and report to hidden bases in the countryside. Every man was issued with sealed orders (other organisations including the NFS were also issued with secret orders) to be opened only in the event of an invasion. These lists included details of potential local collaborators, such as chief constables and Justices of the Peace as well as some rank-and-file police officers. Intelligence sources in the German-occupied Channel Islands had reported that police officers had been susceptible to collaboration, and the British government had no intention of a repeat of this in mainland Britain. Simply put, collaborators might have to be executed if there was a risk of them helping the enemy. Interestingly, chief constables were responsible for the Home Guard in some areas of the country, and most police stations had an arms cabinet as well as a pistol within easy reach of the duty sergeant.

Most of the AU volunteers worked in the countryside and were specifically selected for their local knowledge, their country skills (hunting, for example) and the ability to use a weapon. The men, who were trained at Coleshill in the Vale of the White Horse, Oxfordshire, operated in small groups from disguised bases, which were often underground. Some of these bases remain hidden to this day, not least because they were so well hidden, and many volunteers took the knowledge of the locations to the grave. Their role was to disrupt and destroy the enemy's supply chain, to kill collaborators and to take out strategic targets, and because they were unable to tell anyone about their activities, they had to disguise their true activities. Often, members did this by pretending to belong to the Home Guard, which explains why in post-war years these units have often been incorrectly referred to as the Home Guard Auxiliary.

Here, then, in remembrance of the AU members from the New Forest, is information about the clandestine patrols upon whose services the nation would have called in the event of invasion.

Avon Castle Patrol (inauguration date unknown)
This patrol was part of Group 1 in Hampshire which was commanded by Captain A.J. Champion, also Area Commander (AC) for all the West Hampshire groups. The Assistant Commander (AAC) of Group 1 was Lieutenant L.D.C. Ayles.

The patrol names for the west of Hampshire and the New Forest have been identified from National Archives file, WO199/3391, but are not divided by patrol. The nominal roll gives the surname, initials, Identity Card (ID) number and address, together with date of birth. The patrols have been arranged according to the addresses and ID card numbers around known patrol leaders. This means the allocations may not be completely accurate. Some men, particularly those from the Ringwood area where there were several patrols, could not be allocated with any confidence to one patrol or another, so are listed here.

Name	Date of Birth	Occupation		Died
Sgt Sydney Leonard Moss	26/08/1893	Antiques		1980
Pte G.E. Jones	27/07/1904			
Pte J.A. Frampton	03/12/1899			
Pte Albert George Frampton	18/08/1909		Joined HM Forces May 1943	1976
Bertie D. Brumwell	26/07/1922		Joined HM Forces April 1943	
Frederick W. Canning	27/10/1922		Joined HM Forces April 1943	
Wallace W. Dyson	10/06/1913		Joined HM Forces April 1943	
Wallace W Dyson returned to Unit June 1943			Re-joined HM Forces June 1944	
H.A. Green	12/02/1909		Joined HM Forces April 1943	
Peter Thomas Parkin	03/01/1924		Joined HM Forces Sept. 1943	
A.F. Wiseman	10/06/1916		Joined HM Forces April 1943	

Sydney Moss was an antique dealer from London who moved to Avon Castle in Ringwood during the war. He was promoted to second lieutenant in July 1944 and full lieutenant in August of the same year. G.E. Jones is also said to have lived at Avon Castle, although it is thought the accommodation address given was a timber merchant's offices, part of which was rented out.

In the nominal roll, addresses are normally rubbed out, having been written in pencil in case of changes when men leave the unit. However, parts of the original address are often still visible and these, together with the ID card numbers, which include a geographic code and the position in the register, which appears to have been completed in unit order, allows patrol allocations to be made. In this case it appears that a large part of the patrol went into the forces together. It can be speculated that this was because they shared a common occupation, which ceased to be exempt from call up, particularly since they are of different ages. Given that all appear to have had an Avon Castle address, perhaps they all worked in the timber trade.

Brockenhurst Patrol (inauguration date unknown)
This was part of Group 2 in Hampshire, commanded by Lieutenant G.B. Ash. The AAC of Group 2 was Lieutenant G. Forward.

Harry Burt lived in a forester's cottage at South Weirs. Arthur Warr is listed as a casualty and left the unit in October 1942. However, 'casualty' is a military term, and it does not necessarily mean that he was injured in any way. While most other transfers and departures are given details, this has no details at all. Nothing more is known about the other men in this patrol other than they all resided in the Brockenhurst area.

Name	Date of Birth	Occupation		Died
Sgt John James C.K. Slightam	29/03/1894			
Pte Harry J Burt	04/04/1925	Forester		1994
Pte Harold Frank Emm	13/06/1899			
Pte A.E. Fisher	04/08/1911		Probably Arthur	
Pte R.J. Wells	12/02/1921			
Pte J. Moseley	14/11/1910		Posted 3rd Bn HG May 1944	
Pte Arthur Eric R. Warr	23/02/1921		'Casualty' October 1942	1975

Burley Patrol (inauguration date unknown)

The patrol was part of Group 1 in Hampshire; it was commanded by Captain A. J. Champion. The AAC of Group 1 was Lieutenant L.D.C. Ayles.

Name	Date of Birth	Occupation		Died
Sgt John William Shutler	09/06/1891	Garage owner	Possibly ASC	
First World War	1968			
Pte F.W. King	04/09/1899			
Pte Walter John Marchant	03/08/1893	Gardener	Joined September 1942	1959
Pte F.T. Rolfe	23/01/1897		Joined March 1943	
Pte Edward Hartley Summerell	09/06/1902		Joined September 1942	1987
Pte Frank F. Finch	16/11/1890		Joined June 1943	
Pte Frederick William Carpenter	03/06/1900			

The Burley patrol members were older than the average age of the members of the other Auxiliary Units because all of them had fought in the First World War. Jack Shutler ran the garage on Burley Street and his two brothers also worked in the village, one with a garage and the other at the livery stables. A number of the men listed joined later, according to the AU nominal roll. While sometimes this can be inaccurate, it does suggest that there were other men who formed part of the patrol prior to this, yet their details have not been recorded.

Shortly after the war, Brian Marchant was taken by his father, Walter, to see the Operational Base (OB) in woods just outside Burley. He describes a hidden hatch, with steps down to a fair-sized room with wooden bunks and a table. Forestry Commission employee Ken Harding recalls being asked to take his digger and excavate and destroy the bunker. It was constructed of steel sheets and was quite substantial, taking a significant effort to break it up and bury it completely.

Cadnam Patrol (inauguration date unknown)
The patrol was part of Group 2 in Hampshire and was commanded by Lieutenant G.B. Ash.

Name	Date of Birth	Occupation		Died
Sgt Henry Rebbeck Green	31/03/1897			1969
Pte Bert Corbidge	18/06/1912			1967
Pte Harold John Crouch	02/07/1912			1985
Pte William Charles May	07/01/1898			1980
Pte Mark George Quinton	08/12/1897			1953
Pte George Ernest W. Smith	31/10/1906			
Pte Arthur Thomas Walker	18/04/1910			

Some men, particularly those from the Ringwood area where there were several patrols, cannot be allocated with any confidence to one patrol or another.

Fordingbridge Patrol (inauguration date unknown)
The patrol was part of Group 1 in Hampshire, commanded by Captain A.J. Champion.

Name	Date of Birth	Occupation		Died
Sgt Albert Chafen Broad	09/12/1889			1957
Pte G.B. Bowles	04/07/1913			1989
Pte Reginald John Fry	04/01/1906			2003
Pte H.E. Harper	06/10/1890			
Pte Frederick Charles Molloy	13/09/1909			1988
Pte A.J. Rogers	30/11/1913			
Pte Edward 'Ted' Rogers	06/08/1923		Joined HM Forces Jan. 1943	2005
Pte Samson L.J. Wells	26/02/1897			
Pte R.F. Young	09/10/1896			

The Fordingbridge patrol comprised of men who lived to the north and west of the Avon Valley area. There was another patrol in another group on the other side of the river, around the area of Hale.

Reginald Fry came from Weymouth, where he had married the daughter of a Church of Scotland minister before the war. He was there when issued with his ID card: the Weymouth code indicates he was a resident in 1939. Returning there after the war, his death was recorded in the town.

The Rogers both lived at the same address, and therefore are likely to have been brothers.

Fritham Patrol (inauguration early 1940)

The patrol was part of Group 2 in Hampshire, commanded by Lieutenant Ash. Captain Champion was the AC for all the West Hampshire groups.

Name	Date of Birth	Occupation		Died
Sgt Bertie Benjamin Smith	24/01/1904	Forester	Took over from G. Forward	1966
Pte William Charles Gulliver	28/8/1899	Forester		
Pte W. Thorne	19/08/1900	Forest worker		
Pte Allister Thomas Holloway	17/12/1902	Forest keeper		1967
Pte A.H. Holland	12/02/1912		Joined HM Forces May1944	
Pte Charles Albert Peckham	11/10/1896		Posted to 8th Bn HG	

The Fritham Patrol was started by Gerald Forward, who was almost certainly the patrol's sergeant from its creation until he was promoted to Assistant Group Commander in April 1944. He later recounted some of the details of this time in a privately published autobiography. Gerald was an agister (who assisted with the management of the stock owned by the commoners of the Forest) with specific responsibility for the welfare of free-ranging animals, and with his brother Hubert covered the 93,000 acres of the Forest during the war. He recalled how he was initially approached by a staff officer, who circled the subject at some length before asking him to find the men to form a patrol. This was apparently quite early in the war, possibly July to September 1940, and certainly after the renaming of the LDV on 22 July 1940.

Bertie Smith, Bill Gulliver, and Allister Holloway all occupied well-known forest-ers' cottages in the Forest (Holly Hatch, Bramshaw Wood and Coppice of Linwood respectively). These were official residences that came with the job and formed part of the unique structure of the New Forest. It is likely that the rest of the patrol were in similar occupations.

One of the patrol's OBs was a caravan that had been completely buried, with a dis-guised entrance and in 'a part of the Forest which was difficult to get to'. This cara-van belonged to the Crosthwaite-Eyre family, well known in the New Forest, with various members of the family representing the area as MP, as Official Verderer (the verderer's role being to protect and administer the unique agricultural commoning practices in the Forest) and during the war as Commander of the local Home Guard. Gerald Forward spoke to John Crosthwaite-Eyre, whom he knew was involved in similar work – although it is not clear if he knew how much (John was pictured at Coleshill House at this time) – and one afternoon the caravan was carefully hitched to a tractor and driven off, after John's staff had gone to lunch. It was buried by the following morning.

The patrol also had a more typical corrugated iron shelter, the wood for this being acquired from one of the Forest bridges! This is thought to have been in Bramshaw Wood but no longer exists, as it was dug up by Gerald Forward for use as a pigsty after the war. Gerald reports that the AU trained with regular soldiers, possibly a Hampshire Scout Section, as well as being sent on a training course; it is most likely that this was a patrol leader's course at Coleshill House.

Just prior to the caravan episode, Gerald Forward and John Crosthwaite-Eyre made their own grenades. It is probable that this was when the Home Guard had little more than Molotov cocktails and shotguns.

These grenades were made of cement contained within brown paper and filled with metal debris such as nails and tacks, with a piece of cord as the detonator. Gerald remarked that these were probably most dangerous to the user! A cache of them was discovered after the war at The Warrens, the Crosthwaite-Eyre residence, and the police were called since it was not immediately apparent why they were there. After the war, Gerald Forward was elected as a verderer, and was awarded an MBE for this work in the 1974 New Year's Honours list.

Lyndhurst Patrol (inauguration early 1940)

This was part of Group 2 in Hampshire, commanded by Lieutenant Ash with Captain Champion as the AC. The AAC was Lieutenant Forward.

Name	Date of Birth	Occupation		Died
Sgt J.H. Adams	03/02/1894	Forester		
Pte George Ben Broomfield	28/02/1904	Forester		1981
Pte Henry Charles Barnes	18/08/1892			
Pte Frederick C. Core	07/08/1880			1946
Pte Edward Augustus Soffe	31/08/1901			1965
Pte E.H.S. Wilson	03/04/1919			
Pte J. Collins	29/03/1895			
Pte Lionel Benjamin Wren	29/6/1888	Keeper	Posted to 9th Bn HG Jan. 1943	1948

Sergeant Adams and George Broomfield both lived in foresters' cottages, Denny Lodge and Lodge Hill respectively, so they were most likely to have been employed in that role. Lionel Wren was a keeper, an official appointment that merited a mention in the *London Gazette* in 1936.

Ringwood 1 Patrol (inauguration date unknown)

The patrol was part of Group 1 in Hampshire, commanded by Captain Champion, with the assistant commander being Lieutenant Ayles. The Probert family remember both Champion and Ayles being involved.

Name	Date of Birth	Occupation		Died
Sgt Leslie Charles 'Elsie' Probert	16/11/1900	Butcher		1988
Pte John Rutland Probert	06/07/1923	Butcher's assistant	Joined August 1941	1967
Pte R. Pritchard	15/05/1911		Joined June 1943	
Pte William S. Stephenson	02/10/1904		Joined April 1942	
Pte William Charles Crutcher	09/10/1906		Joined June 1942	1980

Leslie 'Elsie' Probert was a butcher with a shop on Southampton Road, Ringwood, alongside Woolworth's and with a pillbox outside. Leslie's nickname came from the sound of his initials. Some of the patrol's supplies were reportedly kept at the butcher's shop where the family lived for the early part of the war. These included the rum jar, which was dropped and smashed by Leslie's fourteen-year-old son, Peter, who remembers the trouble he got into! John Probert was almost certainly Leslie's eldest son, who helped in the shop and joined the unit when he reached the age of eighteen. He was not eligible for call up, apparently because he had flat feet, so he served with the AU instead. John was usually in charge of the shop as Leslie, who was also a meat agent for the Ministry of Food, spent much of his time travelling all over Hampshire, including the Isle of Wight. Both father and son seem to have been quite secretive about what they were up to and rarely mentioned it, even after the war, and then only in vague terms. It was said that a requirement of AU membership was the ability to swim the river in full kit. This surprised Leslie's children, who did not think he could have managed this.

Bill Stephenson was the local chemist. His shop was three doors down from the Proberts' butcher's shop.

R. Pritchard is not known for certain to have been a member of the patrol, but in the nominal roll his address has been switched with John Probert's, their names being next to each other in the handwritten roll. This suggests they were in the same unit, as the men seem to have been added to each alphabetical page in unit order.

William Charles Crutcher is not remembered by the Probert family by name, but Mary remembers an incident where one of the patrol members was accidentally shot in the foot while in the OB. Her mother was not best pleased that a man had been hurt and said they were nothing more than stupid schoolboys! William Crutcher put in a claim after the war for a disability pension, something he could only have done if he had been injured during training.

There was an underground bunker in the vicinity of Hangersley Hill, which Leslie's daughter learnt about when she was confronted at the breakfast table one morning. Her father had seen her in the area with a soldier the previous night while he was training at the OB, and he took her to task over the matter. Peter Probert recalls that there was also an underground bunker in the woods near Somerley House. It is known that there was a unit there, so the men may have trained together.

Patrol targets are likely to have included the airfield at Ibsley. The patrol is known to have trained at Avon Castle, as did other local patrols. The Proberts are known to have had revolvers and a knuckleduster, as they took these home. Detonators, hand grenades and ammunition were stored in a garage near their house. They also used thunder flashes in training.

Bill Stephenson became a president of Ringwood Rotary Club after the war, an honour also achieved by three other members of AUs from the Ringwood area: Ray Withall, Ted Geary, and Ted Harvey.

Ringwood 2 Patrol (inauguration date unknown)
This patrol was commanded by Captain Champion.

Name	Date of Birth	Occupation		Died
Sgt Arthur Charles Hoskins	29/09/1911		Joined May 1942	1951
Pte Edward Ernest Geary	01/03/1909			1995
Pte Frederick Samuel Geary	20/12/1904			1972
Pte Clarence Jack L. Hanham	20/04/1905		Joined June 1942, known as Jack	1976
Pte George P. Gale	11/04/1911		Joined Sept. 1943	
Pte Raymond Alfred R. Withall	29/09/1911			1980

Fred Geary worked in the family butcher's and grocer's shop; Ted Geary was his brother. At the start of the war, he was just over the age for call up, and he is said to have had a minor heart attack as well, so he joined the LDV. He did not speak of his involvement in AUs but talked about having been in the Home Guard. June Bentley, his daughter, recalls that he enjoyed going out 'with the lads' training on a Sunday morning, although they usually ended up in the pub, drinking or playing darts. He told tales of how on exercises they had captured another platoon or been captured themselves. But, of course, it was never his fault.

George Gale had moved from Dorset, having probably been a member of a patrol there, possibly Moreton. He is recorded as leaving in January 1942 at his own request, but he did not re-join in Hampshire until September 1943. Unusually, therefore, it appears he served in two AU patrols in two different counties.

David Hoskins, the son of Arthur Charles Hopkins, has his father's papers, which include ID cards that show him as both a member of the OC and the ARP Rescue Party leader at different times. He is listed as joining in mid-1942, yet became patrol leader quite quickly, and had a copy of the usual stand down letter that was issued to AUs in November 1944. David recalled that his father served with Fred Geary, Jack Hanham and George Gale. It has been assumed that Fred's brother Ted and his near neighbour Ray Withall were also in this patrol.

It is thought that the OB was located near Three Tree Hill on the outskirts of Ringwood, in the Highwood and Moyle's Court area. Nearby Ibsley airfield would have been a likely patrol target.

The patrol was training at Avon Castle on one occasion when a German bomber was shot down and crash landed in the meadows close by. According to records, this is likely to have been a Junkers JU88A-4 of 2/KG6, which crashed at Southmead Meadows, near Westover Farm, on 7 May 1943. The patrol also met to train on Fred Geary's 8-acre field just outside Ringwood, close to Moyle's Court. Arthur Hoskins attended at least one patrol leaders' course at Coleshill, and he retained the papers from it. The timetable includes the names of Major Oxenden and Captain Delamere, dating this to 1942 or later, as these officers were elsewhere before this.

David Hoskins recalled his father had weapons and ammunition in their larder, and behind paint tins on the top shelf of the garden shed were boxes of grenades, time pencils and tripwires.

After the war, Fred Geary demonstrated his explosives training on occasion. His daughter remembers a large hole being blown in the lawn one fireworks night as he set off some left-over detonators. His son recalls seeing one or more hand grenades in a drum of oil in the workshop (soaking in oil is one way in which to deactivate cordite).

Ringwood 3 Patrol (inauguration date unknown)
The patrol was commanded by Captain A.J. Champion; AAC of Group 1 was Lieutenant Ayles.

Name	Date of Birth	Occupation		Died
Sgt. Joseph Maitland Roger	24/06/1912			1991

Only the patrol leader is known for this patrol. There were other members, but the home addresses overlap with those of the Ringwood 2 Patrol, making it difficult to know which men were in which unit. Unusually, the patrol leader appears only to have joined the Home Guard in July 1942, so it may be that there was someone else before him.

Since both Captain Champion and Lieutenant Ayles came from Ringwood, it is possible that one of them originally commanded this unit.

Ringwood 'C' Patrol (inauguration date unknown)
The patrol was part of Group 1 in Hampshire, commanded by Captain Champion.

Name	Date of Birth	Occupation		Died
Sgt Joseph Maitland Roger	24/06/1912			1991

All the comments for Ringwood 3 Patrol are applicable.

Somerley Patrol (inauguration date unknown)
The patrol was part of Group 1 in Hampshire.

Name	Date of Birth	Occupation		Died
CSM John Harry Burrett	17/04/1908			1969
Pte Arthur William Hudspith	21/04/1910			2002
Pte William Alexander Rabbets	01/10/1909			1985
Pte R.B. Rowson	23/02/1906		Joined Feb. 1943	
Pte F. Warwick	14/8/1888		posted to 8th Bn Hants HG Dec. 1942	
Pte S.W. Warwick	11/09/1921		joined Gren. Guards Mar. 1943	
Pte Vivian John Debben	09/10/1928			2004
Pte E. Rands	07/08/1896			
Pte N.H.M. Jones	12/02/1896		posted to 8th Bn Hants HG Mar. 1943	

These men were all living on the Somerley Estate near Ringwood or nearby at Blashford. It is likely that there were other patrol members who have not yet been identified. Company Sergeant Major (CSM) Burrett would probably have been involved in the administration of the West Hampshire AUs however, he was still listed as the patrol commander soon before the end of the war.

A picture of William Rabbets can be seen via the online link in the Reference Section.

In the 1980s, an underground bunker typical of the type used for an AU OB, was found on the former RAF Ibsley site, which was part of the Somerley Estate. This base has subsequently been destroyed by gravel extraction. Airfield construction did not start until late in 1940, and it is possible that the OB was in place before it was known that the airfield was to be built; there were other defensive anti-aircraft gun-sites nearby.

It is likely that a second OB was built elsewhere on the estate. There are reports from other Ringwood patrols about an underground base on the Somerley Estate. Many OBs had concealed entrances that were secured with various locks, catches and 'booby' traps.

West Hampshire and the New Forest

Patrol names for his area have been identified from National Archives file WO199/3391 but are not divided by patrol. The nominal roll gives the surname, initials, ID card number and address, together with date of birth. The patrols have been arranged, according to the addresses and ID card numbers, around known patrol leaders. This means the allocations may not be completely accurate. Additional personal information such as first names and dates of death have been added using the 1911 census, Ancestry.co.uk and FreeBMD.com. Some men, particularly those from the Ringwood area where there are several patrols, could not be allocated with any confidence to one patrol or another.

Name	Date of Birth		Died
Pte Ronald J. Gardner	20/06/1915		1997
Pte W.J. Lewis	13/07/1902		
Pte J. Mitchell	18/7/1899	Transferred July 1944	
Pte Maurice William Pelling	12/10/1910	Joined HM Forces, April 1943	1975
Pte A.J. Coward	26/09/1904		
Pte Robert Plenderleith	13/09/1911		1983
Pte Albert Edward Cobb	14/08/1902	left c.1942	
Pte Richard Attwood	20/7/1896	Posted 8th Bn Hants HG May 1943	
Pte Bryan Herbert S. Guy	12/12/1913	Nurseryman	1997

J. Mitchell was transferred to Devon Auxiliary Units when he moved to Newton Abbot in July 1944. Bryan Guy was a nurseryman at Belle Vue Nurseries in Ringwood, which still operates today. His daughter was friends with Mary Probert, daughter of Ringwood A's patrol leader, but she is certain he was not serving with her father. If you have any information regarding the above named, please contact the team at Coleshill.

Fortunately, AU members were never called upon, yet they trained and were ready for the day when invasion might come. At a moment's notice they would have been able to face a tried and tested enemy. As the enemy fought to gain ground, the AUs would have engaged in such ruthless tactics as were necessary to protect their territory, with the advantages of local knowledge, determination, and surprise on their side.

It is only in recent years that the AUs have started to gain recognition for their place in the nation's wartime history, although many records and details of precise roles remain embargoed until the year 2045.

Spetisbury Auxiliary Patrol 4 (C A R T)

SECRET

HAMPSHIRE DIVISION

G.S. MEMORANDA NO. 18.

477/G/1
21 Nov 41

1. Road Blocks

Instructions with regard to the correct method of erecting road blocks are attached at Appx 'A'.

2. Disposal of Students in the event of "Active Operations".

Instructions for the disposal of students on courses in the event of active operations are contained in W.O. letter 43/Misc/6895, sufficient copies of which were forwarded under this H.Q. letter S/471/Q dated 8 Aug 41 for distribution down to units. Further instructions on this subject dealing with students attending courses at Sn Comd schools were published in G.S. Memo No. 15 dated 14 Oct 41.

In many instances units are failing to comply with the instructions laid down in the W.O. letter quoted above. The necessity for strict compliance with the terms of those instructions is re-emphasised, especially with regard to the details required to be forwarded with all students attending courses.

3. Home Guard H.Q. Signs.

Ref G.S. Memo No. 16, para 4, dated 21 Oct 41, and G.S. Memo No. 13 para 6, dated 19 Sep 41.

Authority is given for all Home Guard Headquarters higher than Battalions, to have a tactical sign. The sign designed for Zone Headquarters (see G.S. Memo No. 16, para 4) will be used.

4. Damage to Property.

At Appx 'B' is published an Exercise Instruction issued by 1 Cdn Army Tank Bde in connection with a scheme in the NEW FOREST.

Attention is drawn to this as being a first class example of the use of the lighter vein in putting across instructions which are apt to be treated as routine and therefore somewhat perfunctory.

5. Pre - O.C.T.U. Training.

(a) R.E.

Detailed arrangements are now completed for pre-O.C.T.U. training in a 6 weeks course at No. 2 Training Bn, R.E. of all candidates for Royal Engineers O.C.T.Us from all arms of the service.

(b) R.A.S.C.

Other ranks of R.A.S.C. who are recommended for commissions are to attend pre-O.C.T.U. training at R.A.S.C. Mobilisation Centre.

6. Infantry Company Commander School.

The above school situated at ANGLESEY was disbanded with effect from 27 Sep 41.

7. Formation of an A.A. Division at Small Arms School (Hythe Wing).

Plans are being made to form an A.A. Division to replace the Sniper's

/Division.....

Home Guard Notes (AC)

The local paper kept everyone informed.

12

Personal Anecdotes

From diary notes, recorded interviews and telephone conversations, the Forest during WW2 is remembered by several of those who were there, either as locals or as serving personnel.

Mr Brian Bushell wrote,
I was posted as an Instrument Repairer to number 125 Newfoundland Night Fighter Squadron at Hurn Airfield and at the time, they were flying Mosquito aircraft. My quarters were in a Nissen hut amongst a large area of rhododendron bushes on the far side off the Parley to Christchurch main road. Due to the distance across the airfield to the various dispersals area, we were issued with bicycles. These were to also to prove very handy on other occasions such as visits down to local places like Boscombe and Bournemouth. I occasionally attended performances at the Boscombe Empire featuring the model, Jane of the Daily Mirror, who appeared 'in the flesh' so to speak. A stage full of nudes, but they were standing like statues, as had to be the case in those days, because of the censorship laws.

In about August or September of 1944, the 125 Fighter Squadron was transferred to Middle Wallop airfield, near Andover, Hampshire.

Mrs G Walker remembers,
'I was in the Women's Auxiliary Air Force with an operation Mosquito Squadron when in February 1944 they went to carry out the attack on the prison at Amiens. It was called Operation Jericho. With the second front looming, we were then sent off in different directions and I was sent to RAF Calshot. I was amazed at the change from a busy squadron life, to almost the rest camp situation I found at Calshot. However,

it was such a thrill travelling from the bottom camp to the spit head to see the castle and the magnificent Sunderland Flying Boats gently rocking on the light waves in the Solent, alongside the High-Speed Launches (HSL's) of the Rescue Service. I loved the countryside around and when I was duty driver, I used to take baskets of carrier pigeons from the lofts to travel on the early train from Fawley railway station. We also went to

Landing craft assembled in Nearny Southampton (EVA)

the local pub in Fawley, for evening drinks. That's us WAAFs and the airmen from the base. Occasionally when we girls had days off, we went cycling over to Lyndhurst about 14 miles away to have afternoon tea in a lovely little tearoom.

One of my little jobs was to go to collect the local padre from Blackfield to conduct service at the camp on Sundays. When visiting Southampton on 'Swamps' as we called it, we saw many units of soldiers camped under trees almost the length of the journey'

Mrs Barbara Ashton (nee Kemp) now living in New Jersey, USA remembers,
My father was the local policeman at Colbury on the Lyndhurst Road, and I remember one of his most unpleasant jobs was going out at night to finish off New Forest ponies that had strayed onto the road and were hit by cars during the blackout. They were able to wander all over in those days and the car headlights did not pick them out.

Every night about 3 o'clock, we trudged across to the shelter at the big house across the road and I can remember searchlights lighting up the trees and the hum of German planes overhead. Mum would always make us a cuppa when the All-Clear siren sounded. One night a bomb dropped at the bottom of our garden. I remember the whistle as it came down. Fortunately, I had asked my brother to get into my bed that night and it was just as well because some shrapnel landed on his pillow where he would have been sleeping.

One Sunday morning something quite dramatic happened. The siren went and Mum called us from play seconds before a disabled German plane machine gunned along the Lyndhurst Road and across our lawn. People going to church had to jump in the ditches and it was lucky no one was killed or injured. I don't know what happened to the aircraft.

One unexploded bomb on Hunters Hill about half mile away went off when my brother was on the toilet, and it blew him out into the hall. That was quite funny I suppose, and you had to have a laugh whenever

A surviving Nissen Hut photographed in the New Forest (Marc Heighway)

you could back then. Dad came home one day with a parachute from a downed German plane and my aunt was able to make some lovely underwear and nighties for us all. Many Tank convoys came through on their way to the coast and one day my brother and I were riding our bikes home from playing in a local quarry. I told my brother to get off his bike, which is what mum had told us when the Tanks were on the road. Soon after, a huge Churchill tank swerved and when I looked round, I couldn't see my brother. Fortunately, he had seen the Tank coming and he jumped from his bike and ran into the woods. A good job too because his bike was flattened. The Tank crew was unaware of what had happened, but fortunately a dispatch rider saw me crying and stopped to help as he had seen what had happened and saw the flattened bike too. My mum had quite a shock when my brother went home on the back of this motorbike. We never got a new bike out of it!

Our biggest treat was when a NAAFI van overturned outside our house, and we were able to help ourselves to Mars bars and other sweets that we rarely saw due to rationing. Sometimes, we used to stand outside and watch the dogfights over the area and the Ack Ack guns shooting. When the magnesium plant at Marchwood was hit it burned for three days I remember. We took the train to Brockenhurst for school, but they were delayed many times due to troop trains going through. We liked the Yanks best as they threw out gum and chocolate for us. It broke up our hockey match on one occasion as the train passed our playing field at Brockenhurst and we were showered with sweets thrown out by the soldiers. My dad and the local men would sleep in the haystacks and hedgerows at night and were prepared to fight if we were invaded. I don't ever remember being afraid and I gave my parents credit for that. Just before D-Day there

were Mulberry Harbours and Land-
ing Craft in Southampton Water and
all-around Hythe.

Although we were not far from Beau-
lieu, we never really saw the planes
taking off and coming back. We did
however meet a lot of the burned
airmen on the bus that we went to
school on by then. The airmen were
staying at Marchwood House, where
they performed pioneering surgery

A diverted aircraft crashes at Holmsley, wartime
date unknown (AC)

on burns victims. The men were encouraged to travel on the buses and meet with peo-
ple to help with their confidence. Although some were horribly burned, I can remem-
ber mum telling me not to stare. We did feel so sorry for them.

In the New Forest, there was an increase in the number of troops using the area
for training. Local people were used to seeing soldiers arrive and depart at regular
intervals as Alan Howe recalls. '*When we did a bit about the local history at school,*
we learnt that even before the First War, there were training camps here. We now saw
a lot of soldiers and sometimes, Tanks, out everywhere and in some areas, well you
couldn't go down some lanes because they stopped you. We heard guns going off, you
know rifles. Dad had a shotgun so I knew it was a different sound and other times you
would meet soldiers coming out of the woods all made up with camouflage. A couple of
years or so after the war, I was speaking to a retired Police Officer. In conversation, he
told me that the troops knew they were training for war and some used new weapons
and there were a lot of 'experiments' going on in some of the training sites'

From the diary of the late Alan J Mclean of South Africa,
I will never forget our arrival. We were numbers 31 Squadron and 34 Squadron of the
South African Air Force attached to 205 Group, Royal Air Force at Holmsley Airfield,
Hampshire. I asked the Flight Sergeant who was responsible for servicing our B 24
Liberator, where the nearest town was. He said it was Christchurch about 5 miles away
and I asked how me and my pals, could get there. Quick as anything, he said, 'Harpers
Taxi' and he gave us the phone number. When the taxi arrived, it was a Ford 10, and
we could only squeeze in four people. There were eight of us and when we asked, the

chap he said he could not take us and return for the others, because his petrol ration had run out. So, I explained the situation to the Flight Sergeant and his response was 'No problem'. With that he came up with a jerry can of 100 octane aviation fuel and filled the tank of the Ford! Easy, wasn't it?

Mr Harper took us to a pub called the Kings Arms in Christchurch I remember. At Holmsley Airfield, which in our opinion was a very friendly place by the way, we enjoyed five-star luxury compared to what we had been used to. In our smart Nissan hut, we had real beds, proper mattresses, a stove for heating and some washing facilities in the same block. Marvellous and very happy times'

Life was always interesting if not very scary at times, but one of the compensations was that as Air Force types we always attracted lovely girls to go out with. I was still quite young, so this was quite special really.

We flew mainly at night, so the day was spent preparing for this with briefings, sorting out kit, reading up and so on. One of the saddest memories I have is watching helplessly as my closest friend was shot down.

Elsa Hastings was a member of the Women's Auxiliary Air Force, based in Hampshire.
I was Corporal 2053120 Goodhead E, a member of the WAAFs. I served from 1941 until 1945, in the first years as a Flight Mechanic and later as a Fitter IIE posted to 102 Squadron Number 4 Group. For a time, I was stationed at RAF Beaulieu airfield attached to the AFEE (Airborne Forces Experimental Establishment). I had been posted before to a site in Lincolnshire but one January, the whole place was transferred out, planes, personnel, vehicles, if it could move or be moved, it went. We arrived in Hampshire to find the whole area covered in deep snow and on the Beaulieu airfield it was frozen solid. Regardless of rank or title, if we could not do our own work, we were issued with shovels and put on detail to dig out a runway because flying was crucial to our experiments.

Our accommodation was the next shock. The Nissen huts were bitterly cold and infested with earwigs which dropped onto our beds every night. It was so bad that to try and save ourselves from these creatures, we had to put cotton wool in our ears and elastic bands round the cuffs and ankles of our pyjamas. To make matters worse, our sleep was often disturbed by the New Forest ponies that rubbed themselves against the outside of the thin-walled huts. They did that when they were itching and trying to relieve the discomfort. Instead, they made us very uncomfortable.

Because of the frozen pipes, camp water had to be bought in by bowsers however, this was only used for the kitchens and the camp sick bay. We had one metal bucket in our hut, and we filled this with snow which by the time it had thawed left a little water. This we used as best we could for flushing the toilet. We learned to clean our teeth with snow and the mixture of snow and toothpaste resulted in a mouthful of froth which was difficult to get rid of! When the eventual thaw set in, we were gradually able to get on with the work we were sent to do. As D-Day was drawing nearer, our Commanding Officer called all NCOs to a meeting. We were told that the planned invasion of Europe was imminent and whoever was Duty Officer that night would be excused. It was me; I was Duty NCO!

The station was of course very active over the entire period of the D-Day Campaign, but later things settled down quite a lot. I was released from the service in the August. In some of the local pubs I was taught bar games including shove halfpenny which I had not come across before and drinking the local cider was always something to remember. Ann Parnaby recalls the case of one local 'foster-mum' who was both surprised and saddened by the children she looked after.

They were two young lads, the Wood brothers, and the foster mum found it upsetting when she discovered the lads had their clothes all sewn together. The jackets sewn into the pullovers then the pullovers were sewn into the vests with the trousers sewn into the underpants. No one knew when they last had a change of clothes and if the clothes had been sewn together to stop them from being taken off the children. After the children were bathed and put to bed, the foster mum peeped in on them to make sure they were both OK. The lads were not in bed and upon investigation, she found them rolled up in the carpet and laying under the bed. She asked why they were sleeping under the bed and was told that 'Mum and Dad sleep in the bed, we sleep underneath, and that's what we do at home'. It was assumed they perhaps came from one room accommodation and had other family members sharing. It was very sad in any event'

Myrtle Smy (nee Lush) talks about the chatter on the school bus.
The boys and some of the girls used to take bits of shrapnel to school to show off what we had found after the raids. There was much discussion on Marvin's bus about the

raids the night before and who saw what. What was hit, who saw the first dog fight, who saw a plane come down and how many German planes were shot down. One morning in contrast there was a lot of subdued talk about the local searchlight battery which was hit with loss of life.

One day a German bomber swooped really low down over the river and let a string of bombs go before pulling up over the trees and heading for home The plane was so low that from the gardens, we were clearly able to see the pilot. We had seen the enemy, a man flying his plane like our chaps flew their aircraft over Germany.

Later when there was a camp near our house, I used to watch the Sergeant as he showed his men how to strip a Bren gun down and re-assemble it. The cook there used to dish some of us kids, helpings of pudding. The men used to sit outdoors and eat. When there was a raid or when Officers arrived, we made ourselves scarce and flew off like rabbits through gaps in the hedge. We fetched and carried full and empty tea mugs to and from the cookhouse to the crew at the gun site. Then we were allowed to sit up on the gun and look through the sights and turn the handles, with help from one of the men, to swing the gun around or to raise and lower the barrel of the gun.

I was quite good at repairing socks, so the soldiers used to give me darning to do but it took me a time to finish each pair. I was not that quick. Then I used to sketch pictures of girls from magazines and the soldiers tucked them into their wallets and off they went.

Joyce Wilkinson (nee Maton) of Thorney Hill had just turned sixteen when war was declared. She lived within a few miles of where she was born and where she experienced life on the Home Front.

My Dad, Edward who was always known as Ted, and Mum Irene were country dwellers through and through. Dad was a builder so he has a responsible job in terms of war work and so he had a reserved occupation. Later in the war he was working on the big airfield at Holmsley and then went on to become clerk of works when the aerodrome had been completed.

Mum was a professional cook who worked locally and obviously in wartime this proved invaluable because she was able to make the best meals out of the rations we had as well as produce we were able to get locally. There were always rabbits and chickens and eggs of course so we were able to supplement our diets and really, we ate well, and we were healthy for that. I was employed on a local farm doing a lot of the basic but very essential jobs. My work too was a reserved occupation and we put in long days because there was always so much to do. I used to cycle to start work at about six o'clock in the morning and although we were supposed to finish at four or five in the evening, it was always much later than that in the summer months.

We used to have get togethers in the Women's Institute Hut at Thorney Hill. We would have tea, but no coffee of course because we couldn't get any. We had soft drinks too, probably just lemonade, but I can't remember. My family took in an evacuee for the duration of the war. We became friends although she was younger than me, almost like a younger sister. Sadly, she died in a car accident some years after the war.

I met my husband to be who was a cook with the Royal Air Force. It was my job to collect 'swill' from some of the local military establishments and it was while visiting one of these places that I first knew Albert. Dad used to invite some service personnel to the house for a meal and a bath. That was something civilians used to organise for service people stationed nearby. Anyway, Albert was one of the chaps who used to come over to the house so of course I recognised him, and we began chatting and that's how we became friends and eventually husband and wife. After the war Albert was able to get a job as chef in a local youth hostel

Myrtle Smy again.
People were taking about gas attacks and wondering whether we would have gas dropped on us. Nothing much seemed to happen in the early days after war was declared but I often wondered when I played in the local woods or field on my own would I suddenly see German soldiers coming to fight us. If there was gas, how would I know because no one would warn me? I thought too about coming home from school to find that my house had been bombed and I would have no mum. All these sorts of thoughts were going round in my head, but I was not scared for all that. Later on, evacuees came to stay with us. They had lice and used to wet the bed.

My Dads job was as an air raid warden, and this involved walking for miles around lanes and woodland paths checking that the blackout blinds on the houses were closed up and not allowing light to show. He used to knock on doors to let people know he was about and sometimes, he used to come home laden with apples and bottles of home-made wine. So that his walka-bouts could be sorted out into a route, the paths were named after London streets with signs nailed on to the trees. I remember walking down Shaftesbury Avenue to Oxford Circus on many occasions! When the Army were camped there, we never ventured into the woods because it was a bit scary, and I am sure we were not supposed to go there anyway.

Joyce Wilkinson on the land, towards wars end (Wilkinson)

Les Lewis recalls,

'*Suddenly there seemed to be a lot of men and women in uniforms. Army, Navy, Air Force, there were Nurses, more Policemen and of course Air Raid wardens. All the important local buildings began to be surrounded by sandbags and there were soldiers standing guard with rifles. We soon got used to the barrage balloons hovering above us, but at first the sight of them was pretty scary. Dad was in the Navy and sometime in the summer of 1940 he was invalided out because he was suffering from shell shock because of his ship being torpedoed. I remember seeing him walking up Bedford Street carrying a stool he had made from raffia while he was having therapy at Haslar Hospital. Sailors were holding him under each arm and carrying his kit because he was still so unwell. A few weeks later the first air raid took place while my mum, my brother and I were out shopping. We had to go into a shelter under one of the shops and we were given a helping hand by a Policeman. He told mum that he would keep an eye on my brother's pushchair which we were not permitted to take into the shelter. When the raid was over, the Policeman told my mum that a bomb had fallen on a pub which was not far from our house. We had to rush home because dad was there alone, and he was still very ill. We had not expected to be away from him for so long. I was quite frightened and confused by the way people were rushing about and talking quickly to each other. There were bells ringing all over the place and fire engines and ambulances everywhere and the injured people were being treated nearby.*

John Clifford recalls,

My brother was in the A.T.C. (Air Training Corps) and I was in the J.T.C. (now the Army Cadets). Some of the boys were in the Scouts and went on local camps. As a wireless-set operator in the J.T.C. I did more real soldiering than I did in two and a half years in the army after the war out in Germany (when I was but an office clerk in the R.A.S.C.). We went on route marches along the front to Boscombe and back and had exciting times when a great column of cyclists went to Talbot Heath for a day's manoeuvres. We only had blanks for our rifles, of course, but putting a pencil down the barrel made a good substitute for bullets.

The partial remains of a pillbox on the site of former RAF Calshot (Marc Heighway)

In 1944 the school returned to Portsmouth because it was considered safer now for civilians back in the city. So, then my brother transferred over to Bournemouth School, and I started work in the Prudential. It was an easy cycle ride to the Square, but sometimes if the tide was out, I would cycle part of the way along the sands. I think I started at about £70 a year, but then a good lunch at Lyons Corner House was only Is 3d (about 7 and a half pence), and this was usually something like meat patty and vegetables, sponge pudding and custard and a cup of tea. One thing you couldn't do until later in the war, after D- Day when security was less restrictive, was swim in the sea. Until then, many boys used to use the rivers, one of the favourite spots was on the Stour which we reached either from River Way near Jumpers or from Riverside Lane on the Holdenhurst side of the river.

Betty Driver who was from time-to-time touring in concert parties across the area recalled that:
Apart from rationing and bombing and people getting on with their lives, all I can say is that no matter how awful it was, England was like one big family, and we all looked after each other. Even though we had rationing, we did manage to stay well and slim!

John Thornley, late of New Milton, wrote,
Looking back on my early life in those dark days there were compensations as well as hardships. The continual need to make do and mend and the constant threat of death or destruction from German bombs were facts of life. We learned not to complain and

to be content with simple pleasures. Undoubtedly, we were fitter and thriftier with money because we had no chance to indulge ourselves. And because the adults were preoccupied with more important matters, we had the freedom to play and developed naturally which no modern child perhaps hope to enjoy.

Len Lewis again,
One thing that sticks in my mind was the state of the sea and the local beaches. There was a permanent smell of fuel and diesel oil as soon as you got near to the sea and the beaches and sea always seemed to be covered in debris, most likely coming from sunken and damaged ships and planes. Later in the war when we could go on to the beaches, we always had to have a good scrub down when we returned home from swimming and a day on the beach.

Michael Morgan shared this,
I was evacuated from Portsmouth to a reception centre in the New Forest. We went on to Milford on Sea in about mid-September 1939. We arrived at the village school and were later dispatched to various host families in the area. Milford was a small community of about 2,500 people with various military units stationed in the area. I believe the Hampshire Regiment was stationed in the village hall or one of the halls in the village. Dr Barnardo's Children's Homes had a big house on the cliffs during the war. I knew that only after the war during a visit with my new wife to the village.

Meanwhile Maurice Cooper who was also evacuated to the Forest at the beginning of the war reflects how he celebrated VE-Day.
I was away from home for a long time although I had regular visits from my mum. I was with a caring foster family and my experience was positive and helped me as I grew up into adulthood. My foster parents told me what was happening, and we listened to the King speaking to the country on the wireless. The King began by saying 'Today we give thanks to Almighty God for a great deliverance. Speaking from our Empire's oldest capital city, war-battered but never for one moment daunted or dis-mayed - speaking from London, I ask you to join with me in that act of thanksgiving'.

We had lots of local celebrations to join in with. I had no real grasp as to the impor-tance of the occasion, but it was abundantly clear that we were witnessing history in the making and that nothing like this was likely to happen ever again let alone in my lifetime'

Home Guard Camouflage instruction southern HG (AC)

A former Home Guardsman reported that,

'In 1943 there was a crash between two bombers. It occurred because of bad weather initially. Five Canadian (RCAF) 407 Squadron Wellingtons were diverted to RAF Beaulieu from their flying duties. This was about the 13 August, and it was about 5 o'clock in the evening. The weather cleared quite quickly, and they were cleared for take-off to their base in Devon. They climbed to the north of Lymington however, a Halifax bomber of 502 Squadron was flying out of Holmsley at the same time. Because of the proximity of the airfields locally, some circuits overlapped. Holmsley's ran east-wards towards Beaulieu, 9 miles away, and there was an overlap. The Halifax was climbing through cloud on an opposing circuit to the other aircraft and it collided head on with a Wellington flown by Flight Lieutenant Prichard. All personnel in both aircraft were killed in the ensuing explosion and crash as was a civilian, whose house was damaged by the fallen Halifax.

Ann Parnaby

I have fond memories of the Americans and especially their generosity with donating food to supplement our rations

Some of the local Bed and Breakfast places and Hotels were used as billets for the Americans. Many were billeted in Allenhurst Road, Bournemouth, near where we lived, and I remember they held parades in Warren Road.

Dad got to know some of them, especially a chap called Kellcheck and another whose name was Julius. They used to come over to the house for tea and I know that Mr Kell-check had got married when he was 19 and had left his wife and a young baby at home in America. It must have been dreadful for him and the family he left behind. I suppose it was the same for all young men who had been drafted into the Army and had to serve thousands of miles away from home. That's why many families used to take care of the GI's and other soldiers too including the Canadians who were stationed in the area.

Well, we used to have oranges and bananas, such a treat and a wonderful way of cheering everyone up. A taste of the sun and perhaps an indication that life was somehow going to get better. The American chef used to make delicious pastry cases about three and a half inches deep and fill them with plumbed jelly and sultanas. When the chaps left for D-Day, I remember we were given eight tins of this lovely pudding.

They also came to the house and asked my mum how much butter we had. Butter, we didn't have enough margarine let alone butter. They simply gave us packs and packs of butter to fill that larder. They also gave us kid's lots of what they called 'Oh Henry' bars and packets of Lifesavers, a sort of mint fruit sweet.

The Americans were always kind and I remember how when they were on parade, they would pass oranges along the lines until they reached the children standing at the side of the road and I remember once I was watching them from my bedroom window and they made every effort to throw some up to me, but their sergeant was not too impressed.

When they left the area some of the local girls were pregnant, but that's what used to happen in war, you lived for the day and took what pleasure you could for the moment.

People could be dead the next day. I think many of the girls went to America at the end of the war and some married their GI's.

Jack Halsey a US historian who was researching his stepfather's wartime service and the time he spent in the New Forest, provided details of what American service personnel were told to expect.

Britain may look a little shop worn and grimy to you. There's been a war on since 1939. The houses haven't been painted because factories are not making paint – they're making planes. British trains are cold because power is used for industry, not for heating. The British people are anxious for you to know that in normal times Britain looks much prettier, cleaner, neater. Don't be misled by the British tendency to be soft spoken and polite. They can be plenty tough too. The English language didn't spread across the oceans, mountains, jungles, and swamps of the world because these people were 'panty-waists'. Remember that crossing the ocean doesn't automatically make you a hero. There are housewives in aprons and youngsters in knee pants who have lived through more high explosives than many soldiers saw in the last war. If your British host exhorts you to eat up, there's plenty on the table, go easy. It may be the family's ration for a week, spread out to show their hospitality. Most British food is imported, even in peacetime. Today, British seamen die getting convoys through. The British know that food represents the lives of merchant sailors.

British women officers often give orders to men. The men must obey smartly and know it is no shame. For British women have proved themselves in this war. They have stuck to their posts near burning ammunition dumps, delivered messages afoot after their motorcycles have been blasted from under them. They have pulled aviators from burning planes. They have died at their gun-post, and as they fell another girl has stepped directly into the position and 'carried on'. There isn't a single record of any British woman in uniformed service quitting her post or failing in her duty under fire. When you see a girl in uniform with a bit of ribbon on her tunic, remember she didn't get it for knitting more socks than anyone else.

All the WVS canteens were opened up to the Americans when they arrived and they soon realised and appreciated that the women would help darn socks, change shoulder flashes on uniforms and provide information on fetes, dances and events at which the Yanks could 'meet the locals'. Given that some difficulties arose from what was called the private hospitality scheme, introduced to help the Americans acclimatise and to meet British people, the WVS conceived the British Welcome Club which helped to integrate the US servicemen with local communities. In Ringwood, Hampshire for example, forty pilots based at RAF Hurn were invited to a party to meet families in the neighbourhood and visit their homes. It was a great success, wit-

A surviving WW2 NAAFI van at an event in Beaulieu (Simon Thompsn)

nessed by British and American Welfare Officers and the pilots were very loud in their appreciation of their hosts. Subsequently, a list of local families who would welcome enlisted men was given to the authorities and new friendships were forged and maintained, in some cases, long after D-Day.

There was also the NAAFI. In 1939 Britain was at war for the second time in a generation, however for the first time in history, an Army was able to harness a fully equipped and organised canteen service. To meet this commitment, the ranks of the NAAFI staff increased dramatically from a mere 8000 employees to a peak of 110,000. Moreover, the organisations trading establishments rose from nearly 1500 to 10,000 to include the (now legendary) mobile canteens of which there were 900 and there were establishments on 800 ships. Service personnel throughout the New Forest and Hampshire benefitted from regular visits by mobile canteens especially in the months ahead of D-Day when the areas military population increased substantially. As was noted by a local paper which relayed the comments of an unknown NAAFI worker, post war.

One of the pleasures of working at NAAFI was the camaraderie between the staff and the servicemen and women. We got all the usual jibes, you know, things like the rock cakes were hard enough to use for building airfield runways, or the tea was like gnat's pee, but it was always good humoured as far as I remember. I think we all knew that being in the same situation at war, we had to make the best of it. Feeding times were an opportunity to relax and forget your worries just for a while.

A well preserved shelter at Ashurst

13

Evidence of War

For the generation that endured the war years on the Home Front between 1939 and 1945, much of what they had grown up with was lost forever. Whilst that loss was often the loss of family and friends who perished because of enemy action at home and abroad, the loss of possessions and property was a further erosion of the human need for wellbeing, belonging and familiarity.

The loss of property and change to the built landscape was more so the case for town and city dwellers who witnessed the devastation of much that was familiar to them, including schools, factories, churches, and libraries. As William Bowen recorded, 'Whole streets became piles of debris and caches of vivid memories.'

National interest in preserving what was left of our wartime heritage gathered momentum in the 1970s, and since then surviving buildings and other constructions from the period have been restored, many remains have been photographed and the details have been catalogued. In addition, many sites have been taken into public ownership to preserve both the social and built history. Of particular interest to preservationists are former airfield sites and remaining pillboxes, together with associated emplacements. As part of the New Forest Wartime Memories Project, a major survey revealed several previously unmarked and unrecorded sites of wartime occupation. These have now been mapped and recorded, the exercise forming part of a wider fact-finding and information-gathering project which better reveals the wartime role of the New Forest and its people.

Before looking at specifics, we must briefly return to the inter-war years. Much was learnt from the first air raids on Britain during the First World War, and whilst these events were, in context, extreme at the time, they were not in any way an indication or reflection of what was to befall the country just two decades later. By the 1920s, the consensus was that another war seemed remote, and thoughts of prolonged peace ran high. Between 1928 and early 1932, the agreed formula of the Committee of Imperial Defence was: 'It should be assumed for the purpose of framing the estimates of the fighting services that at any given date, there will be no major war for ten years.' Yet it was also in the 1920s that theoretical planning for another 'emergency' was addressed by various government agencies and departments, and consideration was given to, for example, the impact of attacks on the civilian population.

Curiously, some might say, in parallel with this the armed services were being run down. There was no building programme and no plans for wartime infrastructure. In the minds of the public, it was only in the late 1930s that the British government woke up and took notice, when the effects of widespread devastation and destabilisation caused by the bombing of Spanish cities during that country's Civil War became known. Across Britain at this time sites including farm outbuildings, empty factories and other premises were surveyed and registered as potential mortuaries, should the need arise. In the New Forest, many parishes offered their churches for this use. The survey was based on the estimated number of casualties that the country would suffer in the early days of another 'emergency', these estimates arising from think tanks that had met in the previous decade.

Yet there was a contradiction between what the government was doing and what it was perceived to be doing in the face of European and international unrest, between its apparent indifference to war and its intelligence activities, together with the conclusions of various committees. Intelligence-gathering by the government had included enquiring of foreign powers, including Russia, about their experience of war. For example, the Russians were specifically asked about the role of women, as they had been front-line troops for many years. In addition, men returning home to Britain after fighting in the Spanish Civil War were debriefed about their experiences, and much valuable information was gathered.

The Royal Air Force Expansion Programme, which began in 1934, evolved from conclusions reached by and discussions during the late 1920s. Sites for new airfields were surveyed and funds were released to construct a total of about ninety new stations, most being on the east coast of England, facing Germany.

Civil Defence and its role in war, to include air raid precautions, was under the care of the Home Office, a decision that was reached by the inter-war committee known as the Committee on the Co-ordination of Departmental Action on the Outbreak of War (CCDAOW).

The changing social and political climates in Europe during the 1930s brought about a marked change in the mood and attitude of some of those in government, as well as in the press and the armed services. It was not a matter of *if* another war came, but *when*. In contrast to the belief that mass mortuaries would be needed to accommodate the dead from air attacks, however, Winston Churchill felt that carrying out air raids on Britain would be futile, because air raid shelters would be provided for the entire civilian population.

The Munich Agreement of 1938 bought much-needed time for the country to 'prepare for the inevitable', but by the time war broke out in 1939 small local building contractors who had been given Ministry of Supply work, such as the erection of pillboxes and public shelters, were still recruiting labourers to help meet the need. Larger construction companies had been directed to road building and the construction of airfields, in addition to those already required under the expansion programme. A report dated 3 March 1950 about the financial benefits of the war, and the way ahead for planning and construction, stated: 'Many of today's well known national construction companies including Wimpey and Laing's were contracted to build the major airfields at Beaulieu, Holmsley South, Stoney Cross, Hurn and Christchurch.'

At the peak of the airfield building programme, during the early 1940s, it is estimated that as many as 20,000 workmen were employed across the major sites in the New Forest. The largest airfields swallowed up many acres of land with vast complexes that included storage sheds and ammunition stores, accommodation blocks and fuel storage, canteens, hangars, boiler houses, control centres, blast shelters, messes for officers and other ranks, and even a gymnasium and a cinema. These were large and densely built conurbations, almost constituting small towns.

Simultaneously across the county, other building projects included the construction of anti-aircraft sites and underground networks, and bunkers to be used as communication and intelligence centres. Nissen huts, inexpensive prefabricated steel structures made from a half-cylindrical skin of corrugated steel, were erected on concrete bases, often in the grounds of requisitioned properties, to be used by Civil Defence, government and Armed Services agencies. Maycrete buildings were constructed between April and July 1941, although it is incorrect to describe all huts built in a similar temporary style, as Maycrete. The total number of Maycrete buildings amounted to just 525, whereas the main Ministry of Works (MoW) concrete huts, the Orlit and the British Concrete Foundation, were more common, but not however, as common as the temporary brick buildings. Some intact examples, as well as remains, can still be found locally and across the county.

Such a demand for construction on an unprecedented scale led to a shortage of manpower and skills. Recruitment of men from Ireland as well as from overseas, including India, Pakistan, and Canada, resulted in a substantial increase in the workforce, in the tens of thousands. Temporary 'villages' sprang up across the New Forest to accommodate them. Olive Dickson recorded in her diary at the time that 'Every community throughout our beloved land is touched by the boot of the workman. Be it a small concrete slab laid for an Observer's Post or a runway stretching out across once green fields, everywhere is a site for war, that will last for generations, along with the memories and the stories.'

The infrastructure was like a cloth jigsaw, with small and large pieces sewn into a vast picture that was unfolded across the nation. Construction continued apace until 1943, when the last few airfields were completed. Then, on a similar scale, preparations for D-Day began. This included road widening, such as that undertaken at Pilley and on the road between Blackfield and Lepe, the strengthening of bridges, such as those at Beaulieu village and Brockenhurst, the creation of roadside hard standings, slipways, temporary camps including the prisoner-of-war (POW) camps at Setley and additional buildings on existing airfields, including Stoney Cross and Hurn. The Mulberry Harbours were built at sites including Lepe and the Beaulieu River, with up to 10,000 men contributing to the construction and assembly of all the component parts. The entire national infrastructure programme was, depending on which source one uses, estimated as costing between £15 billion and £25 billion, with over £4 billion being spent in Hampshire and the New Forest alone. In truth the actual sums involved are never likely to be known.

In the immediate aftermath of the war, many buildings were abandoned, and others were used for various purposes, including temporary housing for those whose homes had been destroyed in air raids. Requisitioned properties, such as Pylewell House near Lymington and Northerwood House near Lyndhurst,

The road under this railway bridge at Balmer Lawn was lowered to accommodate high density military traffic in the area (M.Knott)

were in most cases returned to their rightful owners. Airfields were stood down and put on a care and maintenance basis, while others, such as Holmsley South, remained in service for a short time until the powers that be decided their fate.

The needs of war had shrunk, but the surplus sites and buildings proved to be playgrounds for some. As a child, Alan Tate recalls:

We used to play in the pillboxes and in the control tower near our home in Ringwood. Today I suppose you would liken it to a film set, but to us as eight- and nine-year olds it was fascinating and fun. Years later, I understood the significance of those buildings and the importance of preserving our history.

That recent history, however, was not something that most of the population wanted to dwell on, and there was, alongside a need for housing and a return to normal life, a desire to remove and destroy all evidence of war on the Home Front. The government of the day budgeted £65 million to remove as many of the wartime structures as possible. People wanted to forget about the war and move forward to a brave new world. That brave new world was built using rubble and hardcore from many of the demolished wartime installations, which themselves had originally been built using rubble taken from blitzed towns and cities. This was recycling on a vast scale.

Wholesale post war demolition continued unabated until preservation groups, many born out of post-war social and cultural changes, urged the listing of buildings such as control towers. Thankfully, public interest in the archaeology of the

Second World War was awakened. Decades later it continues to flourish in part because of instant access to information on the Internet and via social media History platforms dedicated to the story of Britain's Home Front.

One aspect of archaeological study which has contributed significantly to our understanding of the past is LiDAR. This is a technology used to make high resolution maps, and it has written a new chapter in the recording of newly located sites. In simple terms LiDAR is light and radar: the acronym stands for Light Detection and Ranging. It uses ultraviolet, visible or near infrared light to image objects, and it can be used with a wide range of targets, a narrow laser beam being used to map physical features at a very high resolution. LiDAR was one of the tools at the disposal of the New Forest Remembers project team, which operated under the auspices of the New Forest National Park Authority.

It is worth describing this fascinating process at some length. Initially, wartime diaries were read and assessed by the participating Maritime Archaeology project officer, who recorded references to sites within the study area where a named location or a grid reference was given. Relevant information on the site, for example its type, units in occupation, period of use and a short description, were recorded, as were any other notable events that could be identified.

During the Second World War, Britain's armed forces used a mapping system known as the British Modified Military (Cassini) Grid. This meant that the six figure grid references used in the war diaries were totally different to those used by the modern Ordnance Survey, and therefore they needed to be converted to match today's maps. A formula was developed by the Royal Engineers Mapping and Charting Establishment, and the conversion was made with an accuracy of plus or minus 200 metres. It must be remembered that although war diary grid references could be plotted with a reasonable level of accuracy, they were only as accurate as the original reference itself. In total, 595 locations were identified in the war diaries, and these were researched fully before a comprehensive desk-based assessment (DBA) record was written. Some of these appear below – and they are taken directly from the official record for the sake of complete accuracy. This information can of course be further researched and cross-referenced via the websites noted below. In addition, many more sites can be located and explored.

Ashley Walk Bombing Range

The government first suggested the compulsory acquisition of land for bombing practice at Ashley Walk, near Godshill in the north of the Forest in November 1939. The New Forest Verderers received a request from the Air Ministry in December 1939 for a temporary bombing range on the 5000-acre site and the lease was agreed in February 1940. The range was ready to use by August 1940. Ashley Walk bombing range was used by aircraft flying from the Aeroplane & Armament Experimental Establishment (A&AEE) at RAF Boscombe Down. Accommodation for personnel was in hutments erected opposite the Fighting Cocks public house, Godshill. The main entrance to the site was on Snake Road where a guardroom was erected. Two short runway airstrips were laid to provide landing for light aircraft such as Auster. The ranges consisted of several different target areas for bombing, ground attack, mock ship targets, aircraft pens and the Ministry of Home Security target, as well as domestic facilities for crew, two small grass airstrips, observation shelters and towers. Almost every type of aerial ordnance was tested on the ranges from anti-personnel weapons to the 22,000 lb Grand Slam earthquake bomb. The many craters on the site are visible, the crash site of a Lancaster is less so for although at the time it was marked as a secret site there is no obvious evidence of the August 1943 accident. Five Lancaster's were flying over the ranges, the last caught in the slipstream of the aircraft ahead lost control, flew low and one wing clipped the ground. Thankfully, the crash was not fatal for the crew.

Left: Adjacent Ashley Ranges the SAE Millersford site here showing the Garage and Workshop from roof of Photo Block 3 (Vera Storr)
Right: Craters on Ashley Walk near Godshill (NFNPA)

A frequent visitor to the site was a Royal Engineer who was one of a party of Engineers loading target pens with obsolete aircraft.

'We used to take souvenirs off the old planes before getting them off the trailers and into these pens that the aircraft then used to strafe. I was always fascinated by this site which seem to stretch out as far as the eye could see. All sorts of aircraft used to fly over from fighters to bombers. It was fairly remote out there although I am not sure how local people coped with the explosions because I believe there was also night bombing with the site illuminated on occasions. But there was a war on, and we all put up with the changes'

The range was also used extensively throughout the war for the evaluation of rockets and small arms. Activities continued until 1946, but the range was not cleared until 1948. Most targets and facilities were removed, although the Ministry of Home Security target was covered over with an earth mound instead. Some craters were filled in, but many were left open. Today one observation shelter remains, as do features associated with several others, and chalk markings cut into the ground.

Although the range covered a large area the main targets and construction areas were relatively small-scale structures. Many were temporary in nature, for example the air-to ground targets which were most probably made of scaffolding, and therefore they were unlikely to leave any traces on the ground. Ground markers cut into the ground and lined with chalk were left after the range closed and many are still visible from the air today. However, many of the markers were laid in concrete and although overgrown, are in much better condition. The observation towers and ship target are only indicated by concrete footings that are likely to be very shallow in nature. Owing to the high level of explosives dropped here, there is a possibility of live ordnance surviving in the area.

The target areas were Walls 1, 2 and 3, the latter for testing the Barnes Wallis bouncing bomb, Ship Target, Line Target, Air to Ground Target, Fragmentation Targets, and Ministry of Home Security Target also known as the Submarine Pen. This was built at a cost of around £250.000 to enable the RAF, in 1941, to assess the viability of bombing of the huge U Boat Pens in France. Conventional bombing was unsuccessful, and it was not until later in the war that the Grand Slam and Tallboy bombs were used against the Pens with positive results.

The only remaining above ground shelter on the range is an observation hut at Ashley Cross. This shelter, built of brick with a concrete roof, is open at the rear and equipped with narrow observation slits facing towards the Fragmentation Target range. When it was built, a bricklayer arranged a 'V for Victory' decoration to be made into the brickwork on all three exterior walls. The structure is possibly unique by virtue of being built of brick rather than concrete (generally a preferred material on bombing ranges). However, the brick is imported and not of local type. Conservation work was carried out on the building in 2012.

The Armaments Research Department, Millersford, was enclosed in early 1941. The department occupied a near circular area of 650 acres roughly between Deadman Bottom gulley and Millersford Plantation, to the north-east of Ashley Range. Between 1941 and its closure in approximately 1949, the centre was engaged in the testing of static bombs and explosives.

The site consisted of two main areas, the administrative area being close to the B3080 (to the north of the New Forest) and the explosives testing area to the west. (The B3080 leaves the B3078 at Bramshaw Telegraph at a fork. It heads roughly north-westerly along the county boundary before crossing into Wiltshire just after North Charford. After Redlynch it turns westward and goes through Downton, then crosses the River Avon before Wick, where it ends at traffic lights on the A338.) The administrative area comprised garages, offices and the bomb store and magazine, with the explosives area consisting of several pits for detonations, and a number of laboratory buildings, all of which were well protected by turf coverings, and from the latter the explosions could be filmed and assessed.

Searchlight positions were set up across the country throughout the war to illuminate enemy aircraft on bombing missions. War diary research has indicated possibly three positions around Brook Common Golf Course. One is listed as in use in 1940, another in 1941 and the third in 1942. It is possible that these all relate to the same site which was used by different units at different times, and its exact grid reference has simply been misreported in the war diaries. Searchlight emplacements came in many different forms during the war. Some were fully mobile, fitted to the back of trucks with an internal generator. Others may have been in sandbagged emplacements, while some more permanent structures may have had a concrete base and wall along with associated buildings.

Bratley Plain Anti-Glider Obstacles

The NMP (National Mapping Project) has identified this site as a decoy airfield, but the only recorded decoy in this area is at Ridley Plain. It is far more likely that the ditches and banks at this site represent anti-glider obstacles.

In the wake of the fall of France, German invasion became a real threat to Britain. The German deployment of airborne forces had a profound effect on the outcome of fighting on mainland Europe and would certainly have been used in an invasion on the south coast. To prevent gliders from landing, areas of open land such as fields and heathland were covered with materials that would cause a glider to crash. In some instances, poles were erected into the ground, and even obsolete vehicles were used to create obstructions. In some places, banks of earth were erected to make a flat surface more irregular. This was the case at several other locations in the New Forest, including Beaulieu Heath. Aerial photography indicates that these anti-glider defences were made up of long ditches with mounds of earth piled alongside them, and whilst they are still visible as crop marks from the air today, they appear to have been levelled. The NRHE [National Record of the Historic Environment; searchable at http://www.pastscape.org.uk/] only lists one other example of anti-landing obstacles in England, although it is possible that others do survive nationwide.

Anti-tank islands were defensive points, usually centred on major road junctions, bridges or natural features that when obstructed, would delay the advance of German forces, giving time for Allied reinforcements to move to the area. These sites were usually made up of bunkers, roadblocks, trenches, and in the event of a withdrawal being necessary, explosives that could be used to demolish a bridge or road altogether. War diary research indicates that there were seven roadblocks in and around Lyndhurst and Emery Down in 1941. There is also a concrete block in the garden of Clarendon Villa on Gosport Lane, Lyndhurst that may be relevant to those structures. Roadblocks came in various types during the war, including temporary wood and barbed wire obstacles that would not necessarily leave any trace. On the other hand, more complex structures would have involved modifications to the road or the installation of concrete blocks on the verge. It is possible that the structure in Clarendon Villa is an example of this, however, no evidence for bunkers or pillboxes in the Lyndhurst area has come to light. Again, any such installations may have been of a temporary nature and not left any physical trace.

Two searchlight positions at Black Heath are recorded in the war diary research with one known to be in use in 1941 as part of the Southern Indicator and Belts group [this refers to the identification and shooting down of enemy aircraft], and another was in use in 1942. Although the war diaries give slightly different positions for these two, it seems that in all likelihood they were on the same site, and the exact position has simply been misreported in the war diaries. This is supported by the LiDAR survey, which only identifies one potential site on Black Heath. The LiDAR also suggests a large scar that may be trenching and several other pits that may be related.

The LiDAR survey indicates that this is most likely to be a sandbagged or concrete emplacement. Such sites could potentially have left remains below the ground after being removed. Other permanent installations such as cabling for the generator may also be present. Clustered around the site are numerous depressions that may be bomb craters, indicating that the searchlight came under attack from enemy bombers on at least one occasion. The National Mapping Project data lists twenty-two individual records that make up as many as twenty-seven depressions on Black Heath. It is quite possible that these are bomb craters caused by enemy action against the searchlight emplacement. Survey may be able to determine if these are in fact bomb craters or quarrying associated with the searchlight, and further analysis of war diary records may be able to pinpoint an exact date of an attack. However, closer investigation of likely points of defence on the roads into Lyndhurst and in the area around the gun pits may reveal traces of weapons pits and trenches.

Aerial photography indicates that there was a camp at Mogshade Hill from 1944. It is known that Canadian forces were encamped in this area prior to D-Day, and LiDAR survey has revealed the likely location of this camp immediately south of the A31. In the same area, war diary research has indicated the presence of a searchlight position, although a searchlight alone could not account for the level of activity indicated by the aerial photography. However, some structures from the LiDAR survey may represent the searchlight. If this were only a temporary staging camp in advance of D-Day, it is likely that most of the accommodation would have been tented. This may mean that there is little in the way of permanent features such as hard standing or services. However, there may be a great deal of evidence of land levelling to create suitable pitches for tents, vehicle routes and a parade area. A searchlight position may leave a more obvious feature, depending on the type of installation. As this was in all probability an accommodation camp, there is a high likelihood of finding artefacts.

LiDAR survey and aerial photography indicate a system of trackways, trenches, and foxholes at Acres Down and Pilmore Gate Heath and what may be a rifle-range nearby. These are likely to be of Second World War origin although the rifle range may be one of a number built around Lyndhurst in the latter part of the 19th century. Trenches and foxholes in this area would probably have been dug for training purposes as there is no defensive quality to the heath. Many nearby shell holes may indicate that live firing was conducted in the area, and this is supported by the 1943 New Forest Training Map, which indicates that the area was one of the mortars, grenade, and small arms ranges.

The NRHE records 964 examples of Second World War slit trenches of all types, many of which have in fact been removed. The vast majority of these were for genuine defensive purposes at anti-tank islands and airfields or along the coast for example, but practice trenches are rarer. Training trench systems from the First World War are known to survive in Wales, Staffordshire, Northumberland and on Salisbury Plain in Wiltshire. Research and fieldwork at the practice trenches on Salisbury Plain has revealed a great deal of material and personal effects, however, Second World War trenches were not as extensive and were usually a series of unconnected slit trenches and foxholes.

The NMP identifies what might be an Anti-Aircraft (AA or Ack-Ack) battery at Mogshade Hill, based on period aerial photography.

Ack-Ack batteries were first established around the New Forest in 1939 and their number grew during the build-up towards D-Day and during deception operations. AA batteries were either heavy, usually housing four or more 3.7-inch guns, or light, using various numbers of 40mm Bofors guns. With one of the most rapid rates of fire, this versatile light anti-aircraft gun was used on both land and sea for over thirty years and was particularly effective against low flying attack aircraft.

The site at Mogshade is visible in 1946 aerial photography as four equally spaced potential gun positions to the south of Mogshade Hill Camp. As such it may have been built to support this camp. However, no reference has been found to this AA position in extensive war diary research or in existing databases. AA batteries were usually quite extensive sites that included services, magazines, and accommodation. No such structures are visible near these gun pits, indicating that if it were an AA position, it may have been a very temporary deployment. It may be that any AA guns based here were a support unit of the unit based at Mogshade Camp. Further survey work may be able to reveal the true nature of these features and locate any other features that may be associated with them.

Ridley Plain Bombing Decoy

Bombing Decoy number Q160A was a Q type decoy site which was specifically designed to represent an airfield at night. It was built to direct enemy attention away from Hurn and Holmsley South Airfields. It would have consisted of lighting poles arranged in a pattern similar to an airfield's landing lights, powered by a generator in a small command bunker. The site, and its twin site Q160B at Verwood, were listed as being active in the summer of 1942 only, however the NMP identifies what might be an AA battery at Wilverley Post, based on 1946 aerial photography.

The site at Wilverley is visible on 1946 aerial photography as several potential gun positions alongside the present A35. However, no reference to this AA position has been found in extensive war diary research or existing databases.

Aerial photography has shown many features, including trenches, foxholes and possibly structures at Goatspen Plain. War diary research also indicates the presence of a searchlight emplacement (1942) (WO 166/6099) and a Home Guard observation post (1941) (WO 166/1319) in this location. A circular feature at the north-west end of the identified area may be a searchlight emplacement. Training areas that allowed men to practise trench construction techniques were commonplace during the war. There is, however, no record of a live firing range at Goatspen Plain on the 1943 Training Areas map.

Although not a front-line location, further work may reveal information about men and units that trained here before being deployed. Field survey may be able to identify the searchlight emplacement and Home Guard observation post. Recent site visits have noted that the layout of some features may be representative of an organised position rather than foxholes; this may represent the observation post. Aerial photography has shown many features, including trenches, foxholes and possibly structures at Goatspen Plain. War diary research also indicates the presence of a searchlight emplacement and a Home Guard observation post in this location. A circular feature at the north-west end of the identified area may be a searchlight emplacement.

Training areas that allowed men to practise trench construction techniques were commonplace during the war. There is, however, no record of live firing range at Goatspen Plain on the 1943 Training Areas map.

Holmsley South Airfield

RAF Holmsley South was built over the winter of 1941 and 1942 to provide accommodation for units required for Operation Torch in North Africa. It was completed in 1942 as a Class A (permanent) airfield and first used by RAF Coastal Command. Both USAAF and RAF bombers flew patrols form the airfield in 1942 and 1943, before the station was passed to Fighter Command in the build-up to D-Day. The airfield was handed over to the USAAF in July and used by units of IX Bomber Command until October when it was returned to the RAF. It was subsequently used by RAF Transport Command. Regular repatriation flights were flown from the airfield and in September of 1945 and 1946 the airfield hosted public Battle of Britain Day shows. In October 1946, it was reduced to caretaker status (care and maintenance) and later returned to the New Forest.

Even though the construction of Class A (permanent) airfields represents one of the largest war time building programmes of the twentieth century in the United Kingdom, relatively few airfields remain in their original condition or a state of good preservation. Like Stoney Cross and Beaulieu, Holmsley South has been levelled and remodelled, although like Stoney Cross, Holmsley's dispersal bays are utilised in a Forest Holidays campsite. These appear to be original concrete in some cases and re-laid tarmac in others.

The nature of the construction of the airfield and its ancillary buildings means that there is usually little potential for below ground features to be identified. Most of the buildings and features had only surface level foundations and today leave little more than concrete bases. Possible exceptions to this rule include the bomb storage area (described below).

Evidence from Beaulieu airfield also indicates numerous below ground communication and services cables and hatches, which may also be present at Holmsley. In the northern area of the airfield (around Stony Moors woodland) is the bomb storage area of the airfield. The access road to the various stores areas is still evident, and several features have been identified in LiDAR survey that correspond with the various stores and preparation areas. Further investigation of this specific area may identify elements of the various sites established here and the extent of any remains. The NRHE only records ninety-nine known bomb stores in the country, and many of these are not actually associated with airfields.

As with Beaulieu and Stoney Cross airfields, the runways at Holmsley were laid in concrete. When the airfields were returned to the New Forest, the concrete was lifted and removed, but at Holmsley, two significant sections remain at the western end, just outside the Crown Lands, along with original perime- ter track. Further investigation may

Taken by an RAF crew member of the inside of his aircraft, now believed to be Holmsley South (Authors Collection)

reveal in which directions such runways were laid. Holmsley was equipped with a Battle Headquarters that could serve as a point to co-ordinate defence if the airfield was overrun by ground forces. The Battle Headquarters at Holmsley South, located just off the northern tip of the north–south runway, has been largely, but not com- pletely, blocked up with concrete and the cupola has been removed, however the bunker itself appears to remain below ground.

This airfield was one of a number of airfields in the south of England where Nissen Huts and other accommodation units were refurbished, immediately post war, to house families displaced by bombing. This interesting report is from 4 January 1947.

'When Christchurch Town Council receive the next report from their Housing Committee chairman, Councillor W. Bingham, on the conversion of ex R.A.F. buildings at Holmsley South aerodrome into housing accommodation, they should be well satisfied with the progress that has so far been made. In com- pany with Councillor Bingham and the Borough Engineer (Mr. E. B. Wise), a

Christchurch Times reporter visited the 'drome on Tuesday, and found that in little over a fortnight an almost complete transformation has taken place within some of the huge communal buildings. It is the conversion of these larger buildings that the Council are concentrating on first and already a series of flats is rapidly taking shape in each one. There remains, however, a great deal to be done before the flats are ready for occupation, but it is anticipated that within the next few days a greater labour force will be available and that the work will be considerably accelerated.

Number may be reduced.

So far as the conversion of the communal buildings are concerned; the contractors have been working to a plan to construct approximately 46 flats, but it may now be found desirable to decrease the total number in order to make some of them larger. While the biggest proportion of the flats comprise three rooms—a general living room and two bedrooms—there are others with four rooms and some with only two rooms. The buildings are being divided up by means of breeze block walls with a corridor running the entire length, the flats being situated on either side of the corridor. Consideration is being given to the installation of a hot water system, utilising the central boiler house previously used by the R.A.F. A supply of kitchen ranges has already arrived, and as there are no other forms of heating at present the possibility of reinstating some of the slow combustion stoves used by the R.A.F. is also being considered.

A Community Centre?

No decision has yet been reached as to whether the former camp cinema, which adjoins the airmen's mess, is to be converted into living accommodation, but if it is not used for this purpose, it may eventually become a community centre. If the demand arises the Council will make living accommodation out of the former living quarters of the airmen, but at the moment, these Nissen huts, which are of course much smaller than the communal buildings, are not being tackled. It is understood, however, that one of these huts is occupied by a family who were prepared to move in without any alterations being made. From what our reporter saw, it was obvious that the Housing Committee have done a fine job of work under difficult circumstances, and the accommodation they will be able to provide when the work is completed, will considerably ease the housing situation in the Borough pending the completion of the other Council schemes.

Allocation of Accommodation.

Coun. Bingham has asked the Christchurch Times to make it clear that in his report on housing at the last meeting of the Town Council he stated that all the worst cases—not everyone on the Council's housing list—had been circularised with regards to the accommodation that would be available at Holmsley. He also points out that it is not the duty of the Housing Committee to allocate houses. It was their duty to provide them, but the allocation of them was the work of the Municipal Committee'.

The area became known as Tin Town and whilst anecdotal evidence suggests that the community that settled there were all decent folk, some locals sought to tarnish them with an undeserved reputation. Residents were eventually resettled in traditional housing after making the best of the situation at Holmsley. There is no doubt from subsequent anecdotes and diary notes that they created a real community building on the spirit that had seen them through the war years.

Rhinefield Training Area

The roughly triangular area of plain that is bordered on the west by the A35, to the north by Rhinefield Road and the south by Wilverley Inclosure and Burley Road, was recorded as a large Field Firing Area on the 1943 New Forest Training Area Map. War diary research, 33 Army Tank Brigade, has indicated that both infantry and armoured units trained here during the war, and photographs of tank manoeuvres have also been identified in the Imperial War Museum catalogue and in the archives of The Tank Museum at Bovington, Dorset.

The training area has several areas of activity identified in the National Mapping Project data. Additionally, aerial photography has identified further areas of what appear to be shell holes and trenches. Further investigation of these various areas may reveal further detail about the nature of training that took place here. The Training map shows a rifle range immediately east of the Field Firing Area. Additionally, a rifle butt and several chalk markings are visible on historic aerial photography and as still-visible features on modern aerial photography. Rifle ranges tended to have a distinct layout.

Further investigation of this site may reveal the survival of the features themselves, how typical its layout was and further evidence of the activities taking place here.

The area of land north of Wilverley Inclosure shows evidence of numerous shell holes or foxholes and what might be trenches. However, given the use of tanks on these ranges, it is possible that some of the shell holes are in fact gun pits.

Wootton Bridge Depot

Aerial photography indicates what may be a military depot or camp immediately north of Wootton Bridge. Given the proximity of a practice range at Wilverley, it seems possible that this was a depot for stores or ammunition for use in training exercises.

As with many other depots and camps in the New Forest, it is likely that any structural remains will consist of building bases. Modern aerial photography does indicate what appears to be a concrete feature in the centre of the area. It is possible that this is also related. Further investigation may reveal the exact extent of buildings and structures in this area and whether the track on the west side is part of the site or another, unrelated, feature.

Hag Hill Anti-Aircraft Battery

NMP aerial photography indicates what might be an AA battery at Hag Hill, alongside Burley Road. The site is visible on the 1946 Aerial Photography as are several potential gun positions alongside the road. No reference to this AA position has been found in extensive war diary research, although there is a reference to a searchlight position in the immediate area and on the Home Guard maps of Major Crofton. The battery is also referred to by Desmond Hollier, a boy who lived in Sway during the Second World War, who remembers that 'We had three Anti-Aircraft guns at the top of our road close by the tumulus near to Marlpit Oak, and another three in an old gravel pit on Hag Hill near to Wooton bridge.'

AA batteries were usually quite extensive sites that included services, magazines, and accommodation. No such structures are visible near these gun pits, indicating that if it were an AA position, it may have been a very temporary deployment or a Light AA position. Further survey work may be able to reveal the true nature of these features and locate any other features that may be associated with them.

Marlpit Oak Anti-Aircraft Battery

NMP aerial photography indicates what might be an AA battery alongside the Bowl

Barrow 800 metres west of Marlpit Oak crossroads. The site is visible on 1946 Aerial Photography records as are several potential gun positions alongside the barrow. AA batteries were usually quite extensive sites that included services, magazines, and accommodation. No such structures are visible near these gun pits, indicating that if it were an AA position, it may have been a very temporary deployment or a LAA (Light Anti-Aircraft) position.

Setley Plain Prisoner of War Camp
POW camps across the country could be incredibly varied. Some were requisitioned buildings, while others operated more as hostels for POWs who were believed to be unlikely to attempt escape: these were most notably Italians. However, the Setley site, which stands alongside the A337, is described as a standard-style camp, one of a number nationwide, built to house Italian prisoners captured in the North African campaign. It was probably constructed in late 1942 or 1943. Many camps were built by the POWs themselves, to a standard arrangement complete with accommodation huts, garden, canteen, sewage facilities, water tower and accommodation and offices for the Allied troops garrisoning the site. The Italian prisoners at Setley worked on surrounding farms and sawmills.

The camp later housed German prisoners, and although some could leave the camp, this was less prevalent than with the Italians. There is anecdotal evidence of a hut being set alight by some of the POWs, although this needs further investigation. Exactly when Setley was closed is not known from the current records, but it is believed to have still housed men in 1947 and it most likely closed when all POW camps in Britain finally closed in July 1948.

The camp was used to provide housing for gypsy families after the war, possibly until the 1960s. There is no record of its demolition, but modern aerial photography indicates that it has been totally cleared, leaving only building bases and the pattern of the camp. Setley is the only recorded 'standard' camp in the study area. The trace of the site is readily identifiable in aerial photography, suggesting that many ground features still survive.

Brockenhurst Anti-Tank Island
Brockenhurst is not referred to as an anti-tank island in any war diary entries but is referred to in the papers of Major Crofton who was a Home Guard officer during

the Second World War. A map included with these papers identifies an anti-tank ditch at Latchmoor and another at the A337 bridge over the Lymington River. Various other positions are marked, but un-labelled. It has not been established if the areas marked on the Major Crofton map indicate if these defences were ever created or were just particular places, for example, houses to be used to defend in the event of an invasion.

Careys Manor

Careys Manor, Brockenhurst, was built in 1888 as a replacement for a much older hunting lodge that existed in the same area. It is possible that the house hosted a unit of Welsh Guards at some point during the war, but its main role was as the Royal Navy Eastern Warfare School (RNEWS). Exactly when it was requisitioned by the Royal Navy and when it was returned to its owners, and indeed whether it was used to train Royal Navy personnel, Royal Marines or possibly men of SOE Force 136 is not clear from the material so far assessed. As with many other requisitioned houses, ancillary buildings may have been built in the grounds. Careys Manor Hotel is still open for business.

Balmer Lawn Hotel

During the Second World War, Balmer Lawn Hotel, on the outskirts of Brockenhurst, was used as a headquarters for various units based in the area. War diary research indicates that it was initially used as HQ for a Royal Marine Division (this may have been the artillery brigade of the Division) and was later occupied by the HQ of the 3rd Canadian Division. In Holland's Wood, which is immediately north of the hotel, there are several features that may be ancillary parts of the HQ.

Large buildings and hotels were frequently requisitioned as HQs for units during the war because they offered space and accommodation for senior officers and for various planning and administrative units, although quite often major changes would be made to interiors to provide appropriate space. Balmer Lawn Hotel is still open for business.

Balmer Lawn Depot

Aerial photography indicates what may be a military depot or camp at Standing Hat near Brockenhurst, which may have been used for the storage of ammunition or supplies. As with many other depots and camps in the New Forest, it is likely that any structural remains will probably consist only of building bases, and as here, modern aerial photography does in fact show what appears to be a concrete feature in the centre of the area.

This archaeology, of course, is not just about the constructed environment and the remains of that environment. It is also about the social impact of the people who came together from all parts of the country and from overseas to share in the common goal of victory and freedom. In doing so, many of them diarised their experiences, shared their stories of home and family, and for a time, they became part of the community and the fabric of wartime life in the Forest. It is about the change of a way of life and the demands made upon everyone, and it is about determination, dedication, and sacrifice. As we rapidly approach the end of an era that will no longer be within living memory, it is vital that we recognise the value of our archaeology, preserving what can be preserved and memorialising that which cannot.

What makes us the generation we are today stems from the resourcefulness of the previous generation that demonstrated, against great challenges, the capability to build and create on an unprecedented scale, unimaginable today, even with all the technology at our fingertips. The legacy of that era lives on in part through the archaeology of bricks and mortar, galvanised steel, and concrete. Our history lies there too.

For further reference about this project and information about sites, please see www.newforestnpa.gov.uk/wwii and http://www.lidar-uk.com/. Please check that the sites you wish to explore are accessible and safe, and above all that access is permitted. It is advisable that information is sought from the relevant agencies, authorities, and private landowners before embarking on exploration. A recommended starting point for information is the New Forest Centre https://www.newforestheritage.org.uk.

Special thanks and acknowledgements are given to Archaeological Desk Based Assessment, New Forest Remembers, Untold Stories of World War II, Final Report, April 2013. Copyright Maritime Archaeology Ltd, Room W1/95, National Oceanographic Centre, Empress Docks, Southampton, Hampshire, SO14 3ZH.

Remembrance at Lepe
(Marc Heighway)

14

Then and Now

Far too often, our wartime heritage is eroded by progress, be it housing estates, business parks or shopping centres. Another control tower topples, another piece of runway is torn up, a bulldozer crushes another temporary brick building.

Some years ago, I was witness to a conversation between an amateur historian and a landowner, after the latter had dismantled a 1942-dated control tower that was an excellent example of its type. After an hour or so, the landowner acknowledged that perhaps he had been too quick off the mark by considering immediate financial gain rather than considering the long-term benefit of preserving a rare piece of the nation's heritage. Sadly, when it was too late, he came up with an idea that would not only have saved the building from demolition, but would also have generated revenue, created jobs and in turn would have created a history experience for visitors. This perhaps highlights a lack of policy when and where it is needed to safeguard not only buildings, but also the memory of all those who served. Immediately after the Second World War, there was a concerted effort to dismantle as much as possible of the infrastructure of the wartime Home Front. Whilst it was practical, for example, to sell off trucks to commercial enterprises to help bump-start the post war economy, and whilst many 'bombed out' civilians took up temporary residence in former POW camps and barrack blocks, a huge demolition programme saw a speedy end to entire installations, many of which had only been built three to four years previously.

The public and the government had had enough of war, and they wanted to look forward, not dwell on the recent past. Moreover, the nation's mindset after years of hardship, rationing and austerity was still to make the best use of what it had through recycling; the example has already been given of the demolished buildings that were used as hardcore for new roads. The programme to rebuild Britain inevitably led to the wholesale destruction of sites that today we would recognise as being of significant historical value. Thankfully, not all was lost: several airfields were given over to civilian use and others became industrial parks. (I mention airfields in particular because of all the wartime developments these sites were the largest, with the greatest impact on the area and within the community in which they were constructed.) It is still possible to stumble upon evidence of wartime activity. By way of an example, I was shown a long length of cabling in a tree, which had been there since 1944 when the telephone lines were cut and the poles were taken away from what was a USAAF ALG (Advanced Landing Ground) airfield, near Lymington. The site returned to farmland after the war, and the copse that had been chopped down to make way for some blister hangars has been steadily regrowing over the past decades.

A few miles away, and a few inches below the soil near a farmhouse, it was possible to locate more cabling; and nearby was a junction box hanging off a wall. A short distance away, a single brick building was just visible through some dense foliage. I was told it had been a latrine! On the front line of defence in the years leading up to and during the war, the New Forest was to become pivotal in the preparations for, and launch of D-Day. Given its geographical location, its varied open and wooded landscape and its proximity to strategic sea lanes, it is not surprising that as long ago as the sixteenth century the Forest was being used for 'military training that will enhance and harden the fighting skills of the men in conflict at home and abroad' as stated in a report archived in the Hampshire Record Office.

It was here that the South Hants Militia, operating from Exbury, trained to defend the south coast against a possible invasion by the Spaniards who, it was thought, would land on the Isle of Wight. Over the subsequent centuries the South Hants Militia, eventually became part of the Hampshire Regiment, then after the Second World War the Royal Hampshire Regiment. The 1st Battalion of the Regiment formed part of the 50th (Northumbrian) Infantry Division and took part in the D-Day landings on Gold Beach on 6 June 1944.

Surveyed by the War Department in the mid-1930s as an area that would again be ideal for use, the Forest had proved its value as a military asset. During the First World War it was a vast holding camp for Allied soldiers heading for the trenches, yet in another emergency the Forest would be used even more exten-

Walhampton near Lymington was a secret OSS base. It is better known today as a public school. (Walhampton School Archives.)

sively to serve the needs of the RAF, the Navy, and the Army. In addition to Tank driver training, small arms training, bomb ranges, SOE 'houses', a vast tented city for thousands of troops with capacity to expand, the building of Motor Torpedo Boats (MTBs), the creation of Stop Lines, a large Secret Army and everything else that comes as part of the package of war preparation and defence, the Forest had twelve airfields operational at the time of 6 June 1944. Only Hurn Airfield, now Bournemouth International Airport, survives, although the former RAF Calshot, with some obvious signs of wartime occupation, operates as an activities' centre.

The New Forest National Park was created in March 2005 and the New Forest National Park Authority took up its full powers in April 2006. It works in partnership with other New Forest organisations to help achieve its two statutory purposes; to conserve and enhance the natural beauty, wildlife, and cultural heritage of the park, and to promote opportunities for the understanding and enjoyment of its special qualities. Whilst much of the landscape we see today has been shaped by man over many thousands of years, the impact of the Second World War has strongly influenced much of the National Park's character, architecture, and landscape. The surviving visible structures of air-raid shelters, installations, former airfields and bombing ranges all play their role. For the full impact of this evidence on the landscape, it is often best viewed from the air either by *Drone photography or from a light aircraft. Now that much of the landscape has been restored to its pre-war use, landmarks such as the former water towers and control towers have been lost, although some buildings such as the Ibsley control tower, are still prominent.

Wartime buildings were once commonplace, but they are now increasingly regarded as rare survivors of a tumultuous period in our history. Because of their important role, they are now being considered for Listed Building status or Scheduled Monument Statutory Protection, and with this in mind the New Forest National Park Authority is working hard to retain several wartime structures by negotiating with land managers and creating Landscape Management Agreements. The National Park Authority has made it a requirement for detailed records to be created when it is not viable or practical to retain wartime structures. By keeping a record such as drawings and photographs, future generations will be able to appreciate the buildings and structures and the vital contribution they made to our heritage. Although a number of temporary wartime military buildings often found new uses after the war and others were moved to new sites or converted for domestic use, new planning requirements include the need for detailed records for any such building that the owners have been given permission to demolish.

Before his retirement, Frank Green, Archaeologist, for the National Park Authority said that the organisation works hard to update public records of Second World War structures and air-raid shelters that have not previously been recorded, through a series of archaeological field surveys and routine site visits.

As part of a major national project, a detailed archaeological survey was carried out on the New Forest coastline and maritime environment. This work increases our knowledge of the Park's maritime sites in Lymington and Southampton Water. For example, work has previously located uncatalogued Luftwaffe aerial photographs taken for the German U-boat division of the Kriegsmarine. Research of the national archives indicates that there is a vast number of documents available for research. Top secret documents about Operation Overlord and D-Day are now publicly available and this material offers a greater insight into the role that the Forest played during the war. The Second World War will always be subject to public interest and research, and it is imperative that we continue to investigate and record how people managed their lives during the war period.

Whilst it is known that the larger country houses were used by the military as operational bases and as hospitals and for institutional purposes, many smaller houses were requisitioned to store important collections from national museums. Many social details about the New Forest during wartime are still cloudy; for example, there is now an initiative to discover how a large party of Irishmen who were building the Mulberry Harbours on the Cadland Estate were housed and fed. Details of this party and similar groups are poorly recorded, and often the only way to find out is to talk to those who were there at the time.

It is vital to continue to promote and encourage local oral history projects to fill in the blanks, not only to understand local traditions, but also to gain personal stories of

A Minewatchers post Lymington Harbour (Marc Heighway)

people's memories about the war years: memories of how people coped with rationing, of bombing and air-raids, what they did in their spare time, or quite simply how the war changed their lives. This will help to build up the type of account that we can all understand the humorous events and the everyday activities of adults and children living and surviving in this tough period of history. We should not forget that the war brought together many people with others from quite different social backgrounds, possibly through their work or by being billeted or lodging as an evacuee. City children often experienced their first taste of the countryside and the freedom and adventure that the Forest afforded them, as well as the experience of developing lifelong friendships and surrogate families. Frank Green again: '*We should be collecting as many memories as we can of how the war affected those who were living and working in the New Forest and how it changed the lives of our parents and grandparents while they are still with us.*' The National Park Authority is just one organisation that is working hard to bring groups and individuals together to protect their wartime legacy because of its educational and historical value.

The words of soldier John Whitmore, written in 1943 are apt:
The Forest is the greatest of all ironies, the gentle running streams, the majestic trees, the breath-taking views, the animals that roam as free as they wish, while men who come here in time of war have no freedom, no majesty, no gentleness, for we are engaged in the destruction of Forest lands with our tanks, our airfields, our camps, and our heavy boots upon the rich earth. And it is in the rich soil of our country that we lay our dead who from this Forest set out to win freedom, their lives then shortened by the bullet and the bomb. Yet in years to come the trees will still grow, the streams will still flow while our history fades beneath the feet of future generations who may ask, what happened here in this place of such enduring beauty.

While Britain may have been militarily secure in 1940, both sides were aware of the possibility of political collapse. If the Germans had won the Battle of Britain, the Luftwaffe would have been able to strike anywhere in southern England, and with the prospect of an invasion the British government would have come under pressure to agree terms. However, the extensive anti-invasion preparations demonstrated to Germany and to the British people alike showed that whatever happened in the air, the United Kingdom was able and willing to defend itself.

The New Forest, on the south coast of England and therefore within range of enemy air power and vulnerable to attack from the sea, had by 1944 become one of the cornerstones of the nation's ability to strike back. As the historian Alan Morris tells us:

The stretch of private beach at Needs Ore is littered with brick work and concrete from the various emplacements and the myriad of smaller constructions which once dominated the shoreline. Debris from the heavily camouflaged AA gun sites can also be found. From the air, as with most of the Forest airfields and installations, imprints left, because of previous substantial defensive usage, can be clearly seen. Evidence of the area's wartime role must be preserved to help future generations, understand what went on here.

An RAF Veteran wrote a poem during a reunion visit with several former Comrades, to the area in 1962:

The ghosts of yesteryear roam across the forest floor.
You hear them on the steps and at the barrack room door.
Hello, who's there, you cry in a startled voice.
There is never an answer, just an eerie noise.

And when you stand on that broken runway.
You will hear a plane fly by, another sortie, another day.
You look skywards there is nothing there, just a vast empty space.
But you are convinced you glimpsed the young pilot's face.

In the distance a telephone rings in a deserted mess room
You run, breathless, get there soon.
But as suddenly as the sound reached your ears.
It was gone, was it real, your doubts are now mixed with fears.

Then passing by along a tree-lined Forest Lane
A man and girl in uniform, to you they seem quite plain.
Riding a vintage motorbike; it's painted military green.
You glance again, nothing there, nothing to be seen.

The spirits of men seem to want to live on
From a far-off age, yet still in living memory for some
They want to remind us of the futility of war.
To remind us of their own sacrifice which they put to the fore
'We went over to the spirit world; we had no choice.
Please remember us, we have a presence, but we have no voice.'

These words seem to sum up some of the experiences of local people, and visitors to the area, who have reported events, hitherto unexplained, some commonly told and others as one offs. During my many visits to the Forest, including an overnight visit to Stoney Cross airfield and an evening spent at Breamore House, I have never experienced anything out of the ordinary. However, stories abound, particularly about the atmosphere on old airfields. Based on details of the many first-hand accounts relayed during my research, there are events and incidents that cannot be explained away, simply, or indeed rationally.

Whilst compiling this title I was fortunate enough to 'meet', via social media, and later in person, a Hythe, Hampshire based man who explained that he was using his time to walk and explore the wartime history of Forest. Hythe is only a matter of minutes distance from the Forest, which is a popular recreation area for local people, more so out of the tourist season. In the early months of Marc Heighways explorations, there were no tourists and because winter had shredded the trees of their leaves and laid barren the landscape it was easy to identify existing and previously unknown sites of interest. Marc has photographed and video recorded many of these sites with links added to his social media group page, New Forest and Hampshire WW2 Heritage. These postings have subsequently generated comments and additional information from those with a shared interest in the subject. The membership of this group page is increasing week by week, a clear indicator that new audiences are determined to carry forward the wartime story of the area as part of Britain's Home Front history. Marc and those that support his social media page will add fresh impetus to collecting anecdotes, recording sites of interest and to documenting the New Forest at War.

WW2 New Forest Discovered

Marc commented;

'During the challenges that the nation faced in 2020, and 2021, like many local people, I started using my free time to exercise and to explore. Living on the edge of the New Forest the opportunity to explore the area's history was too good to ignore. My 7-year-old son and I soon discovered how much WW2 history and heritage the area had, so decided we would start documenting our finds in photos and video. It would mean my son got more fresh air and together we could learn about the New Forest and history. I started sharing what we found online, and soon realised that other people wanted to replicate our walks in the forest, and all the history we had uncovered.

The natural progression was to create a Facebook group so we could share our findings with the community and learn from other people too. I firmly believe that nobody owns history, it's for everybody to find out about. The Facebook group was the natural platform to let people do that. It soon become popular with parents wanting to get their kids out of the house, then developed to local history enthusiasts, people who love WW2 heritage, through to older people, some of whom still had memories of the wartime. I felt privileged to be able to connect different generations and personalities in this way, all of whom have a shared interest.

The group's focus is the discussion of World War 2 sites and history in Hampshire and the New Forest. Members can upload photos, video, memories, historical interest items, personal anecdotes, plus document their own finds and visits. Every day something will provoke discussion and education on the local sites and topics, whilst raising awareness of the amazing history that's still around us.

My view is that with so much of the WW2 heritage in Hampshire and the New Forest decaying or being destroyed, as well as people's memories becoming lost, it's a fantastic place to keep our history alive. I believe the more people who are aware of local sites of interest and history, the better chance they will have to remain standing and supported for future generations to appreciate. For example, I was looking at Luftwaffe aerial photography of a New Forest airfield and could see what appeared to be a practice target range near the airfield. Evidently it was one used by the allies for practice bombing based on subsequent examination of flight log diaries from the era. I walked out to the location to see if there was still any evidence of where it had been scored then chalked into the ground. Whilst measuring the concentric rings, I saw two bombs sticking out of the mud. They were detonated by the police. Having shown the images to experts, *it appears they were unexploded practice bombs that had small charges in them. So, whilst not being large bombs, they could have still caused injury.*

Enthusiasts, amateur Historians, volunteers, Urban Explorers and even the casual observer all have a part to play in keeping history alive.

A Second World War explosive device found by a walker in the New Forest has been blown up by bomb disposal experts. The bomb, thought to be an American shell, was discovered on Ibsley Common, Hampshire, on Wednesday by Trevor Vaughan after he sat down to rest. He said he put his compass down and noticed the needle swinging wildly. He

Hinton Admiral pillbox (NFNPA)

said, 'I saw there was a little crater and I scraped away at the sandy earth, and there it was.' A Navy Bomb Disposal Team exploded the device. After finding it at Newlands Plantation on the common, Mr Vaughan called the National Trust, who notified the police. Ian Bradwell, the Trust's area warden for the New Forest, said, 'The device was in a remote part of the common, but we weren't taking any chances. We blocked off the tracks while the disposal unit dug a hole round it, sandbagged the area and blew it up. Mr Vaughan, who lives at Poulner near Ringwood, said he had been walking across Ibsley Common for about sixty years, since he was a boy. He said 'I did hear that an American aircraft came down around here during the war. Maybe it was something to do with that.'
(Courtesy of BBC Hampshire and Isle of Wight News
For more stories, please see http://www.bbc.co.uk/news/uk-england-hampshire-24806535)

The Forest continues to fascinate historians, researchers, writers, and artists. The Second World War has left a considerable legacy, which manifests itself in many ways. The story will continue, the future of History lives on.

*Before flying a Drone please do check that such an activity is permitted in the area you wish to photograph.

In the grounds of Exbury House ahead of D-Day

Postscript

In August 1939, Alan Brooke was appointed head of Southern Command, and on the outbreak of the Second World War he went to France as a member of the British Expeditionary Force. Brooke returned to Britain, and in July 1940 he replaced Edmund Ironside as commander of the Home Forces. In this post, Brooke had several major disagreements with Winston Churchill about military strategy, so it came as a surprise when in 1941 Churchill appointed him Chief of Imperial Staff. He was to become Churchill's most important military adviser, and he was promised command of Operation Overlord in 1944 – although the role was given to General Eisenhower at the insistence of President Roosevelt.

Brooke's diaries make fascinating reading, especially as he later added to the original notes that he made during the war.

'I considered the invasion a very real and probable threat and one for which the land forces at my disposal fell far short of what I felt was required to provide any degree of real confidence in our power to defend these shores. It should not be construed that I considered our position a helpless one in the case of an invasion. Far from it! We should certainly have a desperate struggle and the future might well have hung in the balance, but I certainly felt that given a fair share of the fortunes of war we should certainly succeed in finally defending these shores. It must be remembered that if my diary occasionally gave vent to some of the doubts which the heavy responsibility generated, this diary was the one and only outlet for such doubt's.

The question of whether the defences that were created would have been effective in invasion is vexed. In mid-1940, preparations relied heavily upon field fortifications. The First World War had made it clear that assaulting prepared defences with infantry was deadly and difficult, but similar defences in Belgium had been overrun by well-equipped German Panzer (tank) divisions in the early weeks of 1940, and with so many armaments left at Dunkirk, British forces were woefully ill equipped to take on German armour. On the other hand, while British preparations for defence were ad hoc, so were the German invasion plans. A fleet of 2,000 converted barges and other vessels had been hurriedly made available but their fitness for purpose was debatable; in any case, the Germans could not land troops with all their heavy equipment. Until the Germans captured a port, both armies would have been short of tanks and heavy guns.

The later experiences of the Canadian Army during the disastrous Dieppe Raid of 1942, American forces on Omaha Beach on D-Day and when Japanese defenders on Pacific Islands were taken on showed that under the right conditions a defender could exact a terrible price from assaulting forces, significantly depleting and delaying enemy forces until reinforcements could be deployed appropriately.

In the event of invasion, the Royal Navy would have sailed to the landing places, possibly taking several days. It is now known that the Germans planned to land on the southern coast of England. One reason for this was that the narrow seas of the English Channel could be blocked with mines, submarines and torpedo boats. While German naval forces and the Luftwaffe could have extracted a high price from the Royal Navy, they could not have hoped to prevent interference with any attempt to land a second wave of troops and supplies that would have been essential to German success, even if by then the Germans had captured a port and were able to bring in significant heavy equipment. In this scenario, British land forces would have faced the Germans on more equal terms than otherwise, and it would only have been necessary to delay the German advance, preventing collapse until the German land forces were, at least temporarily, isolated by the Royal Navy and then mounting a counterattack. Scholarly consideration of the likely outcome of invasion, including that of the 1974 Royal Military Academy, indicates that while German forces would have been able to land and gain a significant beachhead, Royal Navy intervention would have been decisive, and even with the most optimistic assumptions the German army would not have penetrated further than GHQ Line and therefore would have been defeated. Following the failure to gain even local air superiority in the Battle of Britain, Operation Sea Lion was postponed indefinitely: Hitler and his generals were aware of the problems of an invasion. Hitler was not ideologically committed to a long war with Britain, and many commentators suggest that German invasion plans were a feint (a stunt) and never intended to be put into action.

May we never forget.
There are many war graves throughout the Forest including these at Bransgore (AC)

A 1946 aerial view of Camp 65 with the main road to Lymington at right

New Forest Reference Section

If you intend to visit individual sites, do please check in advance whether the land is private, restricted or in public use. We do not recommend you attempt to access land and property without the relevant permissions that may be required. Please be aware that where public access is usually permitted, from time-to-time activities including timber felling, scheduled farm work and ground nesting may mean access is suspended or restricted. Furthermore, please note that the Forest is used extensively by horse riders, and every care must be taken when travelling through the area.

Please also refer to information provided within this book, relevant to other sites and to the appropriate official organisations. When travelling through the area please consider access during the peak holiday season and please use designated car parks. There are accredited camping sites in the New Forest and designated footpaths and tracks.

At the time of publication, I am advised that there are still several organised walks across the Forest that pass by, or through, some former wartime sites of interest.

Airfield Buildings
Expansion period 1934 – 1939 and WW2
Various contractors and sub-contractors including Laing, Wimpey and McAlpine

1934 – Investigation of sites suitable for the construction of Airfields.
1935 – RAF Expansion Programme commenced.
1938 – AIB – Aerodrome Improvement Board created. Wet airfields considered no

longer suitable. Paved runways considered essential. (1938 - RAF Odiham, one of a number of airfields in the south of England, was developed with 2 hard runways.)
1940 – Bomber airfields were being designed with three hard runways
1942 – Standard operational airfields became known as Class A.
1944 – 24 ALGs – Advanced Landing Grounds constructed in the south of England by the Airfield Construction Service. Fitted with either ST (Sommerfeld Track), SMT, or Pierced Steel Plank (PSP).
1944/1945 – Several airfields developed beyond Class A for heavy bomber use.

HUTS (Types)
Produced by various contractors and sub contractors to Ministry of Supply and Ministry of Works specifications

1. Timber Huts were the XYZ Huts and the MoS Timber Huts
2. Half Brick Huts
3. Plasterboard Huts were Laing Huts, MoS Living Huts and MoW Hall Hut
4. Corrugated Iron Huts were in six types known as Igloo Sheds, Jane Huts and Marston Sheds, Nissen Huts, Iris and Romney Huts.
5. Asbestos Huts were the Curved Asbestos Hut and the Handcraft Hut
6. Plywood and Asbestos Hut was the Seco Hut
7. Concrete Huts comprised the AMS Concrete Hut, the BCF Huts, Ctesiphon Huts and Quetta Huts, Maycrete Huts and MoW Standard Huts, Nashcrete Huts and Orlit Huts.

Technical And Domestic Buildings
Included:

Barracks
Gymnasium
Water supply
Sgt Mess and Quarters
Officers Mess and Quarters
Station sick bay
Airmen's dining room
Electrical services
Latrines

Gas decontamination centre
Squash Court
Produce and grocery stores
Guardhouse
Motor Transport Garage
Fire Station
Armourer
Station Headquarters
Operations Buildings

Workshops and stores
Hangers
Huts various
Photographic block
Parachute Drying Tower
Sewage treatment plant

Water Tower
Generator / Powerhouse
Control Tower
Bomb (dump) stores
Airfield defence installations

https://www.rotary-ribi.org/clubs/page.php?PgID=632446&ClubID=460
Airfields of Britain Conservation Trust UK (abct.org.uk)

New Forest Walks, A Seasonal Wildlife Guide.
(https://www.amazon.co.uk/Forest-Walks-seasonal-wildlife-guide/dp/1850589844)
Walks in this guide pass beside or through sites of a nineteenth-century Volunteers Rifle Range near Hampton Ridge, the site of the Armaments Research Department, Millersford, Second World War bomb craters near Pignal Hill, the site of an anti-aircraft battery command post on Yew Tree Heath and a large mound on Beaulieu Heath used as a backstop to targets used during the testing of aircraft machine guns.

New Forest Explorers Guide
(http://www.newforestexplorersguide.co.uk/)
Walks featured here are Brockenhurst's Volunteers Rifle Range, Beaulieu Heath Second World War airfield, the Setley Plain POW camp, and White Moor, near Lyndhurst which was a military training and holding area.

Sources of information about land ownership include the Land Registry Service and local Parish, Town, and County Councils relevant to the area in which the land lies. Another source is http://en.wikipedia.org/wiki/Operation_Sea_Lion_:_The_Sandhurst_Wargame.

New Forest Remembers project
Hundreds of articles, photos, documents, films, and audio recordings relating to the First and Second World Wars.
http://www.newforestheritage.org/
http://www.landregistry.gov.uk/
http://www.newforest.gov.uk/
http://www.newforesttrust.org.uk/

http://www.newforestnpa.gov.uk/
http://newforest.gov.uk/index.cfm?articleid=5197

General George Patton
Had his HQ at Breamore House for two weeks until the Germans announced the fact in a radio broadcast.

Neville Shute, the KING, Winston Churchill
Visited Exbury House

David Niven, RAF Ibsley
Filmed 'The First of the Few' (retitled SPITFIRE in America) with Polish pilots flying actual sorties.

Donald Bennett
Later Pathfinder Air Vice-Marshall, lived in Dibden Purlieu and flew out of Calshot to New York on the day war was declared.

TE Lawrence (Lawrence of Arabia)
Had long associations with Hythe and Calshot.

Other Sources Of Information
(Please note that this is not intended to be an exhaustive list)

http://research.hgt.org.uk/
Details of Hampshire Gardens Trust which lists a number of sites in the New Forest, Hampshire that have wartime connections, although you will have to conduct further research via the Trust or elsewhere.

Children of the New Forest.
The famous American Vogue war correspondent Lee Miller visited the New Forest, and her article Children of the New Forest was inspired by her time there. She lived in England after the war and her home, Farley House, in Sussex is open to the public.
https://www.leemiller.co.uk/

New Forest at War - Revised and Updated by John Leete
Published by www.sabrestorm.com

Ringwood Tourist Information Centre
The Furlong, Ringwood, Hampshire, BH24 1AZ
https://www.ringwood.gov.uk/visitor-information/

The Verderers of the New Forest
The Queen's House, Lyndhurst, Hampshire, SO43 7NH

The New Forest Volunteer Rangers
http://www.newforestvrs.org.uk/forest-history/

New Forest Explorers Guide
www.newforestexplorersguide.co.uk

The Real New Forest Guide
http://www.thenewforestguide.co.uk/, especially the page relating to Ashley Walk Bombing range: http://www.newforestvrs.org.uk/forest-history/new-forest-explosives/ashley-walk-bombing-range/.

New Forest & Hampshire WW2 Heritage / Marc Heighway
New Forest & Hampshire WW2 Heritage | Facebook

RAF Ibsley
www.rafibsley.com

RAF Ibsley Airfield Heritage Trust
www.ibsleytower.info
https://www.facebook.com/RAF-Ibsley-Airfield-Heritage-Trust-326963387314081/

A History of Avon Castle
https://wikishire.co.uk/wiki/Avon_Castle

Lepe Country Park SO45 1AD
https://www:ddaylepe.org.uk

National Motor Museum, Beaulieu
SOE exhibition.
https://www.beaulieu.co.uk/attractions/secret-army-exhibition/
https://archiveshub.jisc.ac.uk/contributors/beaulieu.html

British Resistance Archive
http://www.coleshillhouse.com/
For Hampshire Auxiliary Unit patrols and Operational Bases see http://www.coleshillhouse.com/hampshire-auxiliary-units-and-obs.php

Friends of the New Forest Airfields
https://fonfasite.wordpress.com
The New Forest Airfields Memorial (OS reference SZ 208 987)

The New Forest Centre
Lyndhurst, Hampshire, SO43 7NY
A visit to the New Forest Centre and Museum at Lyndhurst (follow brown heritage signs) is highly recommended, and Lyndhurst is also a good starting point from which to explore the Forest.
http://www.newforestcentre.org.uk/

St Barbe Museum and Art Gallery
New Street, Lymington, Hampshire, SO41 9BH
The St Barbe Museum and Art Gallery, also in Lymington, is also a good point from which to start a tour. It reopened in July 2017 after a £2 million transformation.
http://www.stbarbe-museum.org.uk/

Not all the sites mentioned below are accessible to the public. Explorers are encouraged to establish the status of such sites and private accessibility (if any) with the relevant owners and the authorities. This list is by no means exhaustive, and it is only intended to give a snapshot of some of the interesting sites associated with the wartime history of the New Forest.

NB. Many of the former Second World War airfields display memorial plaques, many of which were organised under the auspices of New Forest historian the late Alan Brown.

Quick Reference Guide.

All Saints Church, Fawley
(Marsh Lane, FAWLEY SO45 1DL)
A representative selection of flags of the wartime Allied Nations are on permanent display. There are several Commonwealth War Graves in the churchyard.
(See also Fawley Refinery at War below)

Ashley Ranges (B3078)
Also known simply as 'The Ranges', this valley straddles the main road between Fordingbridge and Brook in the north of the Forest and was used for bomb aiming practice. Evidence indicates the famous 'Bouncing Bomb' was trialled here. The area was used for target practice for fighter pilots. A track known as Snake Road leads to the remains of the wartime site, which includes marker and observation points.

Bashley
Ossemsley Manor, just outside the village of Bashley, was no. 624 Camp for German POWs. The exact location of the camp within the grounds has not been identified by English Heritage. The 2nd Battalion Gloucester's were accommodated in tents within the grounds in the build up to D-Day. After some time in the 1960s and 1970s as a country club, Ossemsley Manor was divided into flats. No access

Beaulieu Airfield (B3504, from Hatchet Pond towards Lymington)
To the left the Isle of Wight is visible, and to your right the land is open and expansive. This is the site of Beaulieu's Second World War airfield: some brick and concrete remains are clearly visible as are hutments. The site is partially accessible.

Beaulieu Estate
This was requisitioned, and became an SOE training centre, or a Finishing School as they were also known. Each section had its own 'house', with French and German agents being sent to those countries after training. There were over fifty SOE training bases across the country, one of the requirements being that agents were kept separate from each other.

At Hill Top, junction with Exbury Road and B3054, there are some SOE training houses, now in private ownership. Stand at Hill Top with Beaulieu village behind you. The open land to your right was used to create a decoy town to draw enemy aircraft away from Southampton.

A few concealed pillboxes were constructed guarding the bridge over the river in Beaulieu village. They were built into existing houses in some cases, and evidence can still be seen. Note the plate on the side of the bridge, which gives the date it was reinforced to cope with heavy military traffic in the build up to D-Day.

Beaulieu

A permanent Starfish decoy site was created (SU 409 038) to deflect enemy attention away from Southampton. It is recorded as in use between August 1941 and the spring of 1943

Boldre (via A337, St John the Baptist's Church)

Visit the memorial to HMS Hood. The Hood, the largest warship of its time, was sunk on 24 May 1941 with the loss of all but three of the 1,418-strong company, during the Battle of the Denmark Strait. Car parking is available next to the church, which is open to visitors. Please check access by contacting the Church Warden.
St John the Baptist's Church, Church Lane, Boldre, Hampshire, SO41 5PG
http://www.bsbb.org.uk/

Bransgore (from A35, Lyndhurst Road)

A Second World War communications centre was erected here. It was used to direct operations in the Bay of Biscay. On private land and no recent information available as to its condition.

St Marys Church (Commonwealth War Graves)
https://www.cwgc.org/find-a-cemetery/cemetery/39205/BRANSGORE (ST.

Breamore House (A338, Breamore village)

After being requisitioned, Breamore House was used by the military during the Second World War, and for two weeks it was General George Patton's HQ. A landing strip at Breamore, known as Butchers Field, allowed access for light military aircraft. Stables on the estate were used by the local mounted Home Guard. Nearby privately owned Breamore Mill was a fortification on what was known as a Stop Line, which followed the River Avon. There are three pillboxes nearby: see http://www.pillbox-

study-group.org.uk/defence-articles/breamore-mill/ for further details, including locations. Breamore House is open to the public for some of the year; the Mill is not.
Breamore House, Nr Fordingbridge, Hampshire, SP6 2DF
www.breamorehouse.com

Brockenhurst

Careys Manor was the Royal Marines Eastern Warfare School. This may have been an SOE training school for jungle warfare. The SOE in the Far East went by the name of Force 136. Today the building is Careys Manor Hotel.

Christchurch (A337/B3059 junction in Somerford)

Now a business and industrial park, this was a pre-war airfield with a history that spanned about forty years, from 1926 to the mid-1960s. The buildings have now been demolished. The Germans took aerial photographs of this site early in the war. This airfield used SMT (steel mesh track) which consisted of parallel rows of steel wire welded at right angles to more parallel rows of wire. Lengths of SMT were overlapped and held together with clips.

East Boldre

(B3504 on the Beaulieu to Lymington Road, to the left travelling from Beaulieu)
This is the site of a First World War airfield. The village hall is in an original airfield building.

Exbury (Exbury House, via B3054)

This is the site of former HMS Mastodon, a centre for naval intelligence and associated activities. It is close to the crash site of the legendary Exbury Junkers in April 1944, and the nearby Beaulieu River was full of craft in the build-up to D-Day. In the Signallers Office situated in the basement of Exbury House, on the south coast of England, Jean Gadston, a WRNS (Women's Royal Naval Service) was responsible for typing up the D-Day instructions for the Fleet.

Marion Loveland, A WRNS Officer, and an Assistant to the Commodore was stationed at nearby HMS Collingwood.
'The establishment by then was sealed and although there was a false start on June 5th, on the morning of the 6th, I was one of the team that passed orders to the flotilla in the Solent and in Southampton Water and to the Landing Craft in the Beaulieu River to

'sail. It was quiet on 5th June, and I was hoping the next 24 hours would be the same. It was my birthday on 6th June, and I wanted to have a little celebration if I could. It was not to be. All hell let loose when the orders came through from Headquarters, that General Eisenhower had given the GO to the invasion. We relayed the message to the ships which we had to keep in communications with from the time they sailed. My then fiancé went out on D-Day. News came through later that he had been killed'.

Memorials in the grounds of Exbury can be visited when the Gardens are open. Exbury Gardens and Steam Railway, The Estate Office, Exbury, Southampton, Hampshire, SO45 1AZ
https://www.exbury.co.uk

Hatchet Pond (B3504, Beaulieu to Lymington)
The pond was used by the Fire Service, the RAF and the Royal Navy for various water training exercises, and the site is accessible. It is now a popular visitor destination.

Holmsley South (A35, west of Lyndhurst)
Plenty of airfield concrete hard standings remain on what is now a major campsite: the former perimeter tracks are used as access roads. Holmsley is also the site of the New Forest Airfields Memorial.
Holmsley Campsite, Forest Road , Christchurch, Dorset, BH23 7EQ
(use BH23 8EB for sat nav)
https://www.campingintheforest.co.uk/england/new-forest/holmsley-campsite

Hordle (between New Milton and Lymington, Hampshire)
Walhampton House was an Officers' Rest Centre, a cover name for an Office of Strategic Services (OSS) base. It was officially listed as 'USAAF Station 558. Principal US Units Assigned: Det D, 93 SCSRD; USSTAFE'. It is presently a school. The SOE helped establish and train OSS agents before America's entry into the war, giving that organisation the benefit of its experience. No access

Hurn (B3073, Bournemouth International Airport)
A few scattered temporary brick buildings survive. On the perimeter of the airport can be found other remains of wartime infrastructure.
It is recommended you contact the airport authorities for further information.

Bournemouth International Airport, Parley Lane, Christchurch, Dorset, BH23 6SE
http://www.bournemouthairport.com/

Hurst Castle (via B3058, Milford on Sea)

Travel by ferry from Keyhaven or on foot along the shingle spit from Milford on Sea to this fort, which was originally built by Henry VIII in 1544 as part of a chain of coastal fortresses. The castle was modernised during the Napoleonic Wars and again in the 1870s, when two enormous, armoured wings were constructed. During the Second World War, coastal gun batteries and searchlights were installed here. Hurst Castle is managed by Hurst Marine on behalf of English Heritage.
http://www.hurstcastle.co.uk/
For ferry times see http://www.hurstcastle.co.uk/ferries/

Hythe (A326)

Motor Launches and MTBs were built here. The former Husbands shipyard has now been demolished. T.E. Lawrence (Lawrence of Arabia) lived here for a short time. Hythe is shown in German reconnaissance photographs from the early war years.

Ibsley (via A338)

Remains of a control tower (on private land) can be seen from the road. There is a stone memorial in Ellingham Drove and visible are the remains of the end of the original main runway. Other remains can be found but please check who owns the land and details of access.

Lepe (Lepe Country Park, via A326)

There is a magnificent memorial here overlooking the Solent. This is the site of the PLUTO trials, and visitors can see the remains of Mulberry Harbour construction. Troops embarked from here for D-Day. The site has a visitor centre.
Lepe Country Park, Exbury, Southampton, Hampshire, SO45 1AD
www3.hants.gov.uk/lepe
www//https:ddaylepe.org.uk

Lime Wood Hotel, formerly Park Hill (B3056, Lyndhurst to Beaulieu Road)

Park Hill was requisitioned by the National Fire Service (NFS) as a Regional HQ unit and was also used in planning for D-Day in 1944 when the area was part of the Colour Scheme.

Lime Wood Hotel, Beaulieu Road, Lyndhurst, Hampshire, SO43 7FZ
http://www.limewoodhotel.co.uk/

Lymington (via B3504, East End and Pylewell Park)

The site of a Second World War airfield. In the area is a refurbished blister hangar and some farm sheds that were used as debriefing rooms for returning air crew. These can be viewed from the road. No access to the main house and grounds

Minstead

No. 716 Light Composite Company, Royal Army Service Corps was stationed in this village, (which is south of Cadnam, and a few minutes from the main A31 truck road) on 6 August 1944 after returning from Normandy. This was an airborne unit. There is a silver alms dish in All Saints' Church (Church Lane, Minstead) inscribed with the names of thirty-three men of this Company who died.

Needs Oar Point (also referred to as Needs Ore Point, south of Beaulieu)

One of the grassed airfields of the New Forest, Typhoons flew from this frequently muddy site, which was protected by several AA (Anti-Aircraft) batteries. The farmhouse at nearby Park Farm was an HQ unit. Along the shoreline are brick remains, and in some hedges on the farm are strips of Sommerfeld tracking, a lightweight wire mesh used as a prefabricated airfield surface. James (Jimmy) Kyle DFC known as the Abbeville Kid for his successful missions over Northern France, flew from this airfield. No access

Northerwood House (Emery Down, Lyndhurst)

A temporary maternity Hospital for mums evacuated from Southampton and later used by the Army. The site is in private use as apartments. No access

Setley Plain (A337, opposite The Filly Inn)

Between Brockenhurst and Lymington, off the A337. Some hardcore and brick remains indicate the site of the former German Working Party POW camp. Anecdotal evidence suggests some Italian POWs, were also here for a short time. Prisoners worked locally in agriculture and were held here at no. 65 Working Camp, Setley Plain, Brockenhurst. At least one of the German prisoners stayed behind and built a life in Ringwood after the war, and there is evidence to suggest at least ten former POWs stayed in the United Kingdom rather than return home. The site is accessible.

Stoney Cross (via B3078)

Good evidence remains of this airfield, which was originally built on a 500-acre site but was then expanded to 900 acres. There are views from the surrounding roads, and it is possible to walk some parts of the site, and to make some interesting discoveries. Anecdotal evidence suggests that SOE occasionally used this airfield for incoming and outgoing flights carrying Agents from nearby Beaulieu.

Sway, Quarr House, Manchester Road, Sway.

During the war it was no. 645 Camp for German POWs. The house has now been divided into flats. No access

Sway, Meadens Garage

The site occupied by Meadens Garage was a fuel depot and in 1944 was used to waterproof military vehicles in preparation for D-Day.

Totton (Testwood School, via A326)

Wartime use as a training centre for the Fire Service. Home Secretary Herbert Morrison met members of the NFS Overseas Contingent here. Volunteer firefighters from Canada also trained here before supporting the NFS 1942–5.
No access unless possibly negotiated with the site Managers.

Fawley Oil Refinery at War

This is a brief overview of the site at Fawley, a famous landmark on Southampton Water, which is also well known for its striking impact in the East of the New Forest. During World War Two it was a much smaller site, yet its profile was raised with its contribution to Operation Overlord.

The refinery at Fawley on Southampton Water was established in 1921 by the Atlantic, Gulf and West India Oil Company. It was later taken over by the British affiliate of the American Esso company, known as Anglo American Oil Company, although for years it was always referred to as the AGWI terminal. Refining ceased temporarily during the war years and Fawley was used for oil storage.

Refinery defence procedures in case of war had been made well before Chamberlains Peace in our Time speech in 1938. From 1938 the preparations were intensified, and various task forces began on site training in gas detection, first aid, fire watching, demolition, rescue, and decontamination. Air raid shelters were built at key sites in and around the refinery. The old wooden telephone exchange was replaced with a reinforced concrete structure, which also housed the refinery control room. The shelters were linked by telephone to the control room.

A Fire Marshal and a Deputy were appointed in January 1940. When day staff were off duty, night superintendents were responsible for the co-ordination and the supervision of the site.

A number of procedures were in place to warn of air raids Yellow warnings were received by telephone to alert that enemy planes were in the vicinity of or flying in the direction of Fawley. On receipt of the telephone message, it was expected that night duty staff would be at their posts within four minutes. Red warnings were received when the public sirens were also sounded. These warnings alerted that enemy planes were going to be overhead within minutes. Purple warnings were relayed only on site, to warn everyone that an attack could be imminent.

The War Office, not unsurprisingly, ordered that the refinery should be defended. Guards were then positioned around the site with mobile patrols in support. Bofors guns were installed and around the perimeter a mobile 3-inch Anti-Aircraft gun operated however, the crew was later disbanded and redirected to other duties, including Home Guard and ARP. This freed them up to assist with many essential duties on site because 'all hands' were needed. From late 1940 and through 1941, sticks of incendiary bombs were dropped on the site as were a number of HE (high explosive) bombs. Damage overall was not as serious as might have been expected, however All Saints, Fawley did lose its roof in one explosion when a bomb, missed the refinery and fell into the church yard.

By 1942, plants were only operating sporadically added to which, a manpower shortage meant that operators were reduced to what were effectively skeleton crews. These crews had to operate the crude batteries, the treating plants, the asphalt oxidising and all the utility services. Apart from some specialty distillations, the refinery was virtually shut down in early 1943 and was then the responsibility of a caretaker staff.

The site at Fawley was connected, by underground pipeline, to the country's war time oil pipeline network. It became the depot for the PLUTO pipelines which helped to provide fuel supplies to the Normandy beaches in support of Operation Overlord in 1944.

It was decided early in the war that the head office functions, the staff and the company records would be safer, and indeed better served, by moving out of London. Appletree Court, Beaulieu Road, Lyndhurst (now the New Forest District Council headquarters) was identified as being suitable and was subsequently purchased as a war time headquarters. The London staff transferred in September 1939, initially to *Cuffnells Hotel in Lyndhurst while Appletree Court was being made ready for occupation. It was ready within two months and so from November, it served both as offices and living quarters for a number of staff.

Appletree Court remained the headquarters until the Company was finally wound up and its business functions taken over by the Anglo-American Oil Company (AAOC) in 1947.

There were many incidents recalled by staff at Fawley, that caused a mix of dismay and humour, yet despite their somewhat precarious situation at this oil installation, they all did their bit to ensure the utmost safety of everyone on site and all those living in the immediate vicinity.

*Cuffnells was a country house, once the residence of Alice Liddell (Alice in Wonderland). It became a hotel early in the war and later was used by a Searchlight Battery and an Ack – Ack battery. The house was demolished in the early 1950s.

Breamore House was used buy the military during WW2. An airstrip to the left of this photograph was known as Butchers Field Breamore House.

Lyndhurst - Northerwood House

Some of the prisoners at Setley Camp helping with a touring concert party (Betty Hockey)

Evidence of the former Setley POW Camp (Marc Heighway)

Directional Arrow, Ashley Walk Ranges (NFVRS)

This Forest cottage is one of many that the spirits of wartime airmen are supposed to visit (M.Knott)

Lawrence of Arabia,Calshot (Martin O'Neill)

There is a small museum at Hurst Castle which adds to the story of the area during WW2 (Authors Collection)

Major Auxenfans and NCO's at the wartime Garrison (Hurst Castle)

Training for D-Day on the New Forest coast of Hampshire (AC)

Former railway sidings at Worthy Down Camp Winchester
(Marc Heighway)

Hampshire Reference Section

The following information is given as a guide for your further interest and research. It is not intended to be a comprehensive account of the county of Hampshire during WW2. Please be aware that some sites are in private ownership however, making written initial contact about research, may produce helpful responses. Not all sites still have evidence of wartime occupation.

This is a good place to start your research:
Wessex Film and Sound Archive and Hampshire Record Office
Sussex Street, Winchester, Hampshire, SO23 8TH
https://www.youtube.com/user/WessexFilmArchive
https://www.hants.gov.uk/librariesandarchives/archives/wessex-film-sound

Also try local Parish and Town Councils direct, or local History Groups

Portsmouth
This city is now a unitary authority within Hampshire.
Please see below for information.

Southampton
This city is now a unitary authority within Hampshire.
Please see below for information.

BBC News: Hampshire & Isle of Wight
'In pictures: Memories of life and work in the New Forest during WW2'
http://www.bbc.co.uk/news/uk-england-hampshire-24806535

Necropolis Cemetery
WW2 Canadian Firefighters, including the Officer who was killed in Southampton, are laid to rest here.
https://brookwoodcemetery.com/

Hampshire Women's Institute
https://hampshirewi.org.uk/

The Auxiliary Units (AU's), Headquarters Bishops Waltham.
http://www.coleshillhouse.com/hampshire-auxiliary-units-and-obs.php
www.staybehinds.com

Hampshire Group 1
Avon Castle Patrol
Burley Patrol
Fordingbridge Patrol
Ringwood A Patrol
Ringwood B Patrol
Ringwood C Patrol
Somerley Patrol
Unallocated Men Hampshire Group 1

Hampshire Group 2
Brockenhurst Patrol
Cadnam Patrol
Fritham Patrol
Lyndhurst Patrol

Hampshire Group 3
Braishfield Patrol
Hale Patrol
Sherfield English Patrol
West Tytherley Patrol

Hampshire Group 4
Baddesley Patrol
Bishopstoke Patrol
Chandler's Ford Patrol
Swaythling Patrol
Unallocated Men Hampshire Group 4

Hampshire Group 5
Bishops Waltham Patrol
Droxford Patrol
Soberton A Patrol
Soberton B Patrol
Southwick Patrol
Unallocated Men Hampshire Group 5

Hampshire Group 6
Locks Heath Patrol
Park Gate A Patrol
Park Gate B Patrol
Titchfield Patrol
Unallocated Men Hampshire Group 6
Warsash Patrol

Hampshire Group 7
Buriton Patrol
Froxfield Patrol
Langrish Patrol
Unallocated Men Hampshire Group 7

Hampshire Group 8
Chalton Patrol
Clanfield Patrol
Cosham Patrol
Havant Patrol
Lovedean Patrol
Unallocated Men Hampshire Group 8

Auxiliary Units were effectively an underground Secret Army ready to surprise and resist an invasion by the enemy. Working from Operational Bases (OB's) each unit would consist of five to six men. Women are known to have unofficially assisted some Units. Such was the secrecy surrounding this organisation that family and friends of members knew nothing about the role they were involved in. So well hidden were the OB's that many are unlikely to be discovered. A few have been found after years of research although it is known that some were filled in at wars end.

Requisitioned Estates and Houses
This is by no means a complete list of the properties that were requisitioned or otherwise taken over for war use in Hampshire. If you consider that war use included Military staff accommodation, Headquarters Units, Training Centres (various), Rest Homes, Hospitals, Evacuated schools, Strategy Centres, and especially heightened D-Day planning centres from 1943, Fire Service colleges, Ministry of Food offices and sites for the storage of supplies and equipment, it can be appreciated that there was a huge demand for suitable facilities. Reasonably, and based on past and recent research, most large houses and estates in Hampshire contributed to the war effort to a greater or lesser degree.

These include, but are not limited to,
Minley Manor near Blackwater. ATS, Canadian, Australian and New Zealand troops and staff college. (P = private)

Arlebury Park Alresford. National Fire Service Offices, as part of the Colour Scheme. (P)

Broadlands, Romsey. Home of Lord Louis Mountbatten. Open to the public on some days

Hackwood Park, Basingstoke. Hospital facilities and other uses. (P)

Aldermaston Court, Tadley. Auxiliary Territorial Service (ATS) and other uses. (P)

Bramshill House, Hartley Wintney, Hook. Red Cross Penny a Week Fund Centre. Training centre for local HG Units. (P)

Bentworth Hall, Bentworth, Alton. In service with the Royal Navy. (P)

Theddon Grange, Theddon, Alton. POW Camp (P)

Avington Park, near Winchester. For the greater part of WW2, Avington Park was occupied by American Forces developing and planning the personnel and supplies logistics in the build up to, and support services, for D-Day and beyond. (P)

Northington Grange, Alresford. In March 1944 at the Grange, Winston Churchill met General Dwight Eisenhower here for a series of discussions about the high-level preparations for D-Day. At that time, the Grange was occupied by HQ the 9th Div. and the grounds became the main storage depot, food, and arms, for the entire Division. Regimental HQ for 47th Infantry was at 50 Broad Street in the town, easily identified by the Plaque on the front of the house. Troops were under canvas in nearby villages including, Tichbourne and Cheriton, Bighton and Bishops Sutton, as well as the Grange.

Oakley Hall, Oakley, Basingstoke. Housing for children of Royal Navy Officers based in Portsmouth. Now a hotel.

Alton, Holybourne Down, believed to be the site of a dummy airfield. Nearby Lower Froyle, was the site of an advanced radar control searchlight, one of three sites, the others being at Bentley and Odiham. The location of each of the corresponding Anti-Aircraft batteries is unclear at the time of research.

Langrish House, East Meon was used as a base for and accommodation of Canadian Troops. Now a hotel. East Meon was a prime evacuation area for children from Portsmouth.

Hinton Ampner, east of Winchester. Portsmouth Day School for girls moved to this site.

Stanstead House, Rowlands Castle. Used as an Orphanage

Castle Malwood, Minstead was a home for refugee children, run by Barnardos Homes. (P)

Allum Green House, Lyndhurst. Used as a Hospital. The home of Vera Brittain Vera Brittain (spartacus-educational.com) (P)

Hursley House, Hursley, Winchester. British 50th (Northumbrian) Division. Offices for the Design and production management of the Spitfire. American personnel also based here for D-Day. (P)

Aylesfield House, Shalden, Alton. A Flak House (Rest Home air crew from early 1944). This was regarded as the most modern facility in the USAAF Rest Home programme. (P)

Sydmonton Court, Sydmonton, near Kingsclere. US troops were stationed here, including the 3274 Quartermaster Service Corps. (P)

Roke Manor, Romsey, was s USAAF rest home and it is now a research centre. (P)

Stanbridge Earls, Romsey. Aircrew Rest Home, now a private residential complex. (P)

NB
For USAAF combat air crews in the UK, home leave was impossible. The doctors responsible for their well-being, believed the next best thing would be Rest Homes, using the tranquillity, comfort, and freedom from military routine achievable at English country houses or hotels. They were provided with civilian clothes. Uniforms were only worn for evening dinner. A Medical Officer gave emergency care or medical advice. American Red Cross (ARC) girls acted as hostesses, supervising the recreation and dining.

Southern Railway.
The Mid Hants Railway is a preserved steam railway running on a short stretch of former Southern Railway between Alton and Alresford. The Southern Railway line originally from Waterloo to Winchester carried Blitz rubble from London to be used as hardcore at construction sites in Hampshire and the New Forest. Troop trains also used this line. At Alton passengers could change for the Meon Valley Railway line to Fareham. National Fire Service personnel under the Colour Scheme for D-Day detrained at Alresford for nearby Arlebury Park Fire Service Centre. At Alton, the adjoining Station Café is on the site of the original café that served troop trains and it was also a meeting place for locally based Military personnel. (Please also refer to information about Alresford as given elsewhere)
https://watercressline.co.uk/

Airfields and Landing grounds (other) including, ALG's and ELG's
Advanced Landing Grounds and Emergency Landing Grounds.
This site provides a page on every Hampshire airfield, with a brief history.
www.hampshireairfields.co.uk

Odiham. Hook. In October 1937, several high-ranking German Officers, including General Milch were given a guided tour of RAF Odiham. The airfield is still on active military service.

Farnborough. Now a commercial airfield, the original airfield was known as the home of British Aviation.

Hartford Bridge/Blackbushe, Yateley. One of the prime testing sites for FIDO, Fog Investigation and Dispersal Operation, later one of the satellite London Airports and later still the home of Doug Arnolds privately owned Warbird GB collection of various Allied and German aircraft. It is a private airfield and the home of British Car Auctions.

Southampton, Eastleigh, is now a commercial airfield.

Chilbolton, Stockbridge. Now an Industrial site.
Middle Wallop, Andover. Is the home of the Army Air Corps, and the Historic Army Flight.

Lee on Solent. Solent Airport.

Thorney Island. (This site originally had a Hampshire postal address)

Soberton. Meon Valley ELG

Thruxton. Andover, now a Business area and motor racing circuit.

Chattis Hill. Stockbridge. One of the Spitfire dispersed production sites after Woolston was bombed.

Eastleigh RAF Southampton. Now Southampton Airport.

(RAF) Flowerdown. Winchester. YT Listening / wireless site.

Frost Hill Farm. ALG between Kingsclere and Overton. Pilot training on Lysanders. Gosport.

Larks Barrow. Whitchurch

Hamble. Southampton.

Hythe. Southampton.

Lasham. Alton. Commercial airfield and Gliding centre. Memorial at The Avenue entrance

Marwell Hall. Colden Common. Better known now as Marwell Zoo. Between late 1941 and March 1944, Cunliffe-Owen Aircraft used part of the Marwell Estate as an airfield to support the manufacture of its aircraft in Southampton.
Portsmouth. Now an industrial estate

Aldermaston. Tadley (Then, in Hampshire). Now AWE.

Efford. Lymington, private airstrip (littered with debris / obstacles to prevent use)

Worthy Down. (Was HMS Kestrel), Winchester. Still a Military site.

Breamore House. Fordingbridge, Butchers Field airstrip

Across the New Forest and throughout the county of Hampshire, there were decoy sites and dummy airfields such as those at Butser, Hurstbourne Tarrant, Houghton and Holybourne Down. These were created to draw enemy attention away from operational airfields. Designated as 'K' sites for daylight use and Q sites for use at night.

Also refer to Airfields as listed elsewhere in this book.

https://historicengland.org.uk/ contact this organisation regards WW2 crash sites.

Royal Observer Corps posts. (Also referred to in Chapter 4)
Headquarters Winchester.
Atherfield. (IOW). Opened September 1943 at Z454791. Closed October 1944.
Barton. Opened July 1943 at Z.240929. Closed January 1945.
Boscombe/New Milton. Opened July 1943 at Z.711914 (San Remo Hotel roof).
Botley. Opened 1926 U.512133 resighted to U.509147 December 1940.
Brightstone. (IOW). Z.423816 closed 1944 (no opening date).
Brook Bay. (IOW) Opened October 1943. Closed October 1944.
Chandlers Ford. Opened 1926 U.434200, resighted U.423193 April 1939.
Cheriton. Opened 1926 U.580288. Closed July 1940.
Christchurch. Opened September 1938 at Z.149929.
Compton. Opened 1926 at U.775146.
Copythorne. Opened 1926 at U.312154 resighted to U.286161 October 1942.
Exbury/Stone Point. Opened 1926 at U.430002 resighted to U.437017 June 1940.
Whitchurch. Opened December 1937 at O.542179.

(IOW Isle of Wight)
Other ROC posts in Hampshire were located at Medstead, Fordingbridge, Hardley, and Hambledon, Overton, Ringwood, Selbourne and Southsea, Stockbridge, Stratfield Turgis, Upham and Fleet, Odiham, Langrish, Headley/Bordon and Marchwood, Longparish, Lockerley Green, Lyndhurst and Kings Worthy, Keyhaven, Herriard and Kingsclere.

My thanks to Marc Heighway for the additional research.

A useful reference book is *Attack Warning Red* by Derek Wood (ISBN 0356084116)

NB

The Observer Corps became the Royal Observer Corps following support to the RAF during the Battle of Britain in 1940. Where no closing date is given with the above ROC posts, this is because the sites later contained a Cold War Underground Post. (http://www.roc-heritage.co.uk/)

Prisoner of War Camps

Various categories of secure camps for German and Italian prisoners of war.
https://historicengland.org.uk/

Romsey, Gangers Camp, Braishfield Road.
Fareham, East Cams
Alton, Fishers Camp
Alton, Medstead Grange
Southampton, Highfield
Southampton, The Avenue
Bordon, Oakhanger Camp
Popham, near Basingstoke, Micheldever Road
Tidworth, Arena Camp
Tidworth, Park House
Chandlers Ford, Hiltingbury Road
Eastleigh, Stoneham Camp
Church Crookham, Fleet, Haig Lines
Whitchurch, Bere Hill
Larkhill, Amesbury, Fargo Camp
Aldershot, Carfax Estate at Tongham
Aldershot, Willems Barracks
Aldershot, Beaumont Barracks
Aldershot, Puckridge Camp
Whitchurch, Newbury Road

Home Guard Units in the county, included-

3rd	Hampshire Battalion **Basingstoke.**
17th	Hampshire Battalion **Portsmouth.**
18th	Hampshire Battalion **Dockyard Port.**
19th	Hampshire Battalion **West Wight.**
23rd	Hampshire Battalion 37 **General Post Office Unit.**
29th	Hampshire Battalion **Gosport.**
32nd	Hampshire Battalion **Connaught.**
3rd	Basingstoke Battalion Home Guard **Thornycroft.**
11th	Hampshire Home Guard **Eastleigh.**
24th	Hampshire Home Guard **Alton.**
1st	Battalion Southern Railway
2nd	Battalion Southern Railway
3rd	Battalion Sothern Railway
4th	Battalion Southern Railway
5th	Battalion Southern Railway
6th	Battalion Southern Railway
1st	Battalion Home Guard. **Andover.**

Most factories had their own Units or cover was provided by a local town or village unit. Other organisations, for example Fawley Oil Refinery, formed their own units. The Southern Railway had 35.000 employees serving as Home Guard.

One former Home Guardsman wrote that:
We usually had two parades a week. We received instruction's not just on using a rifle, they were old Lee Enfield rifles, but also on the Lewis gun. Grenade practice was always interesting because not everyone was able to throw the thing far enough. Regular guard duties would be around the area, on main roads and bridges and from time to time we would have battle exercises against other local platoons across open land and woodland. Exercises using what were dummy bombs, often caused serious laughter rather than instructional benefit. But we knew that if it came to it, we would know what to do, with the desired consequences for the enemy.

The Home Guard: The Real Story Behind Britain's WWII Dad's Army (www.warhistoryonline.com)
The Home Guard of Great Britain (www.staffshomeguard.co.uk)

Home Guard Ranks

Home Guard Appointment	Equivalent Army Rank
Zone Commander	Brigadier/Colonel
Group Commander	Colonel
Battalion Commander	Lieutenant-Colonel
Company Commander	Major
Platoon Commander	Captain/Lieutenant/2nd Lieutenant
Section Commander	Sergeant
Squad Commander	Corporal/Lance-Corporal
Volunteer	Private

Women's Land Army in Hampshire
https://www.womenslandarmy.co.uk/tag/hampshire

Civil Defence in Hampshire
https://civildefenceassociation.uk/history

Police Service in Hampshire
https://www.hampshireconstabularlyhistory.org.uk

Fire Service in Hampshire
https://www. hantsfire.gov.uk

Hampshire Other
Southampton History
Southampton was one of the country's Blitzed cities, yet the wartime role of this south coast port was extensive, especially in the months ahead of June 1944. A contingent of the volunteer Corps of Canadian Firefighters was based in the city.
https://www.southampton.gov.uk/arts-heritage/history-southampton/spit

Portsmouth History
The world famous Royal Navy port, and during WW2, a newly created tunnel complex under Portsdown Hill became a communications nerve centre. Portsmouth was blitzed yet survived to play its part in the war effort. A contingent of the volunteer Corps of Canadian Firefighters was based in the city.

https://www.visitportsmouth.co.uk/things-to-do/tour-stories-of-ww2-por
https://theddaystory.com/discover/researching-local-d-day-connections/

Gosport History
Gosport The Avenue, PO12 2 JU Civil Defence Control Centre, former ARP reporting centre. Various pillboxes and some anti-tank cubes remain in the area.
Circa 1940/41, a Stop Line was constructed from Portsmouth Harbour, running north of Gosport town to Rowner, at a point near St Mary the Virgin Church., abutting a tributary of the River Alver. The boggy wetland around the Alver, was considered to be a natural obstacle to Tanks however, an anti-tank ditch was dug along the length of the Stop Line and with anti-tank cubes added at the road near Fort Brockhurst. Five pillboxes gave support at key locations.

During the second World War Gilkicker Fort, Stokes Bay was briefly armed with a 40mm Bofors gun. Gun Laying Radar was fitted outside the fort to direct the guns of the nearby Gilkicker Anti-Aircraft gun site. During the build-up to D-DAY, a signals unit occupied the fort and on the 9 June, during the Normandy landings, over 1,000 signals were recorded for the day, with onward routing to over 1300 addresses. Later an average of 800 signals to almost 1,000 addresses were routed via Gilkicker. The fort was the site of artillery exercises in 1953.

Gosport was a prime south coast embarkation port during the war especially in the build up to D-DAY
https://www.english-heritage.org.uk/visit/places/fort-brockhurst/
https://www.gosportsociety.co.uk/
Gosport - Visit Hampshire (www.visit-hampshire.co.uk)

Fareham History
Fareham. The Old Manor House, Wickham Road, was used by the Royal Signals, early war and later by the Admiralty.
Monument Farm, heavy Anti-Aircraft gun site PO17 6AX
https://royalarmouries.org/venue/fort-nelson/

Military Attractions in Hampshire - Hampshire's Military Attractions
(www.visit-hampshire.co.uk)

The following list is a random selection of examples of how the county of Hampshire was impacted by the war, in both a social and military capacity.

Winchester. Cheesefoot Head, Matterley Estate A272/A31 The site of a tented city for troops ahead of D-Day.

Wickham, near Fareham, Wickham Square was a military vehicle park, and part of the one-way military traffic system in Hampshire which was introduced in the build up to D-Day.

Micheldever, off A30 between Basingstoke and Winchester. Andover Road/Brunel Close. Micheldever Station. RAF Oil Terminal.

Northington. Winchester. The remains of a Booster Unit structure for the underground oil pipeline which served airfields, situated off the main road between the village and the A33.

Southwick House. Southwick village, Fareham was loaned, by the owners, to the Royal Navy (HMS Dryad) and later in 1943 it became the forward command post for SHAFE and the planning of D-DAY.

Southwick village. Fareham. Golden Lion pub. Unofficial Officers Mess for senior ranks at D-Day HQ.

Petersfield. Buriton Chalk Pits were named HMS Mirtle during WW2. They were used by the Admiralty for the disposal of unexploded bombs which would arrive at Buriton railway sidings and would then be shunted into one of the site buildings to be X-rayed. Any secret booby traps would show up on the X-ray. Once a mine was declared safe it would be taken to another part of the site to have the explosives steamed out.

Newnham, Hook. Crown Lane. Six young Sappers of 48th Section of the 6th Royal Engineers Bomb Disposal Company, died on August 18th, 1940, while attempting to defuse an unexploded bomb that had fallen on the railway line near Crown Lane, Newnham. The UXB had fallen overnight and due to its location could not be left. The time lapse also meant, as all the Sappers were aware, the UXB could explode at any time. The UXB detonated whilst the Sappers were excavating it, killing all six and injuring the Lance Sergeant in charge. Lance Sergeant Button was later awarded the George Cross for his actions on that day. A memorial plaque at Hook railway station has the names of the personnel who walked from this station to the UXB site. Some years ago, a memorial cross was erected in Crown Lane at the side of the main railway and close to the explosion site.

Bursledon. Manor Farm County Park. Former site of shore station HMS Cricket. Commissioned in 1943. Royal Marines Landing Craft crew training base. Managed by Hampshire County Council.

Alresford, at the entrance to Perins School. An information plaque explains the purpose of the nearby stone blocks.

Lyndhurst. Pats Garage, in Romsey Road, was the site of a British Restaurant. Public catering services, providing a hot meal at nominal cost organised as part of a government scheme across the country.
British Restaurants in 1940s wartime Britain
(https://www.1900s.org.uk/1940s-british-restaurants.htm)

Ower, near Romsey, Paultons (Park) was used as a temporary school for pupils transferred from Portsmouth. Now a family theme park.

Totton. Longdown Estate. Starfish decoy site, part of a network of sites to draw enemy attention away from Southampton. The other sites were at -

Chilworth. Southampton. A Starfish decoy site (2)

Durley. A Starfish decoy site (3)

Botley. A Starfish decoy site. (4)

Nutburn. North Baddesley. Starfish decoy site (5)

Lee. A Starfish decoy site (6)

Botley, an Anti-Tank Island was created at Sherecroft Gardens

Barton Stacey Camps A, B, C and D camps, occupied from 1943, across an area of over 2000 acres of land near Andover. Military Training area. Visible evidence exists.

Hartley Wintney. Hazeley Heath. Tank Testing ramps

Kingsclere, The Crown pub. 3 people died, including 1 civilian, in a shooting incident between U.S Troops and Military Police, towards the end of WW2.

Aldershot. Queens Avenue during WW2 was the most famous and busiest parade ground in the country, running as it did through the centre of the home of the British Army.

Lockerley and Dundridge, near Romsey. A huge US depot with 15 miles of railway sidings. Part of Operation Bolero and later Overlord. The nearby Mill Arms pub was a favourite meeting place for military personnel, and still welcomes visitors today.

Droxford. 1944 meeting between Churchill and de Gaulle on the now defunct Meon Valley Railway. The railway was used by troop trains as well as for carrying military supplies, particularly in the months ahead of D-DAY. The MVR was guarded by Regular Army personal and units of the Home Guard, including the East Meon Unit which carried out regular training along the line.

Bishops Waltham. Beeches Hill. The site of a Y Station listening post, part of the Bletchley Park network.

Alton, on the site of the Waste Centre, A31, east of the town, was a WW2 Cold Storage Food Depot. These depots were always built close to railway lines or siding's.*

Overton. Overton Mills in the village became the wartime base for the Bank of England. 1200 bank staff were relocated. Plans for accommodation were delayed so interim arrangements were made at other locations.

Whitchurch. Hurstbourne Park was temporarily used to accommodate staff from the Bank of England.

Basingstoke. Queen Marys School, Vyne Road, was requisitioned to provide accommodation for Bank of England staff working at Overton Mills

Basingstoke, a WW2 Buffer Food Depot was built in the fields that subsequently became Oakridge and Popley housing estates, north of the town. Local children recall finding boxes of tinned food in the derelict buildings during the 1960's.

Basingstoke. the large area, on Worting Road, from Deep Lane to what is now the West Ham roundabout was the Thornycroft factory which produced vehicles for the War Department in WW1 and WW2. During WW2 the company employed 2500 people, had a 24-hour shift pattern, invented the Terrapin Amphibious Vehicle, and produced field guns, Bren Gun Carriers and over 13.000 assorted wheeled vehicles plus various parts for torpedoes and other military equipment. Much of the wartime camouflage paint applied to the buildings could still be seen at the time of demolition. The factory had its own railway sidings, now buried under a section of the inner ring road.

Romsey, Dean Hill. The site of a major Royal Naval Armaments Depot.

Bordon and Longmoor Military Camps, Canadian Army WW2 with Canadian Army UK HQ at Broxhead House. Also, Longmoor Military Railway.

South Warnborough, near Hook. A Unit of the National Fire Service Overseas Contingent was based in temporary huts in what is now Ridleys Piec.
Off Gastons Lane. Gaston Copse (private land) is the site of a Wellington Bomber crash 4 July 1944. There was one survivor.

Winchester. Bushfield Camp A3090, was a muster point and training centre for military units including US 47th Infantry Regiment, 9th Division.

Winchester. The cellar of 25 St Thomas Street was open as a public shelter. The city hosted an American Information Bureau in Southgate Street (now a shop).

Petersfield. East Meon Road and Droxford Road from Clanfield. HMS Mercury shore establishment was commissioned at the Leydene House site on 16 August 1941. It was a Signal School with crew often exceeding 100 personnel.

Basingstoke Canal and the Aldershot GHQ Stop Line. There is a lot of evidence of canal defences along sections of the surviving waterway
http://www.pillbox-study-group.org.uk/

Hartley Wintney, Hook. Oak Common was a Tank Park ahead of D-Day. Victoria Hall was used as a Red Cross Centre and the Appleton Hall was earmarked as a gas decontamination centre. Douglas Bader learnt to walk on his artificial legs at The Grange, home of his friend, Adrian Stoop a famous rugby player. There is a magnificently restored type 24 pillbox at Phoenix Green.

Ampfield, Romsey. On July 2nd, 1944, five USAAF Pilots of the 50th Fighter Group, based at Carentan, France, boarded a Cessna Bobcat light Transport for a flight to the U.S.A.A.F. base at Chilbolton, Hampshire. The aircraft was never to reach Chilbolton. It developed engine failure on one engine and the prevailing weather conditions of low cloud and thunderstorms made flying difficult. Just after Noon on that July Sunday, the Cessna was seen to crash into the woodland, north of the local church, the pilot steering the plane away from local homes. There were no survivors. You can visit the Memorial in Chapel Wood, Ampfield.

Alresford, Station Road, the Civic Cinema, (demolished) was a regular destination for service personnel in the area. The existing Alresford Community Centre was once the Town Hall and a very popular dance venue for the troops and local people. In East Street was The Tea Pot tearoom, a private house also known as The Blue Door.

South Warnborough, near Hook A maintenance and repair facility was erected here for National Fire Service vehicles. The exact location is presently unknown.

Rotherwick, Hook, Tylney Hall. During the Second World War, Lord Rotherwick's interests came together when Tylney Hall became the Headquarters for his famous shipping line, Clan Line Steamers Ltd. In 1942, three of the Line's Cameron class steamers were requisitioned by the Royal Navy whilst still under construction at Greenock Dockyard and commissioned as -
HMS Athene, an aircraft transporter.
HMS Engadine was also an aircraft transporter
HMS Bonaventure became a submarine depot ship for X-craft.
The Clan Line lost a total of 30 ships during WW2.

Odiham, Totters Lane. Several pillboxes, and an area of Dragons Teeth survive. These were originally part of the network providing cover for the main London – Southampton railway line. On private land, but visible from the lane.

Shalden, (crossroads) Alton, The Golden Pot. Popular with WW2 pilots and crew from RAF Lasham and RAF Odiham and reputed to be one of Hampshire's most haunted pubs. Post war, it has had many owners, with few staying more than a couple of years. At the time of research, the building was empty.

Horndean, Five Heads Road. Storage of military vehicles in fields ahead of D-Day

Basingstoke, Park Prewett Hospital. Some of the original buildings have been saved although new housing developments have swamped the site. A specialist medical unit operates on the site in the grounds of the main Basingstoke and North Hants Hospital. Park Prewett was one of the main American Hospitals in Britain. It was also, a centre of Sir Harold Gillies pioneering plastic surgery unit from 1940. The hospital was served by its own railway branch line which was linked to the main railway network.

Havant, A vast D-Day transit camp was situated south of Emsworth Common Road. The smaller north camp on the opposite side of the road was hit by a flying bomb, after the troops had left. Rosalie Hill was born in Havant in 1940 and later recalled, *I was too young to be scared by what was happening. We were living in my Nans house and there were three families on four floors. One incident was when I wanted to go up to my bedroom and collect my doll. A few minutes after I left my room a bomb dropped on the local library. The blast blew the windows out in our house including the windows in my room. I had a narrow escape from flying glass and debris. People were killed at the library. On a happier note, when we later met the Canadian troops, they were so kind to us and gave us drinking chocolate and lovely red apples'*

Andover, Anna Valley. Messrs. Taskers produced the Queen Mary trailer for transporting aircraft.

Bramshott, Camp Bramshott. Huron and Ontario Camps were located on Bramshott Common near the Portsmouth Road. Superior Camp was located at the Grayshott end of Ludshott Common. Erie Camp was located at Headley Down, in the area now occupied by Heatherland's estate. Connaught Military Hospital was located on Bramshott Common, adjacent to the A3.

Alton, (A32 south of the town) Rotherfield Park. A memorial tree was planted by members of the Museum of D-Day Aviation, for Sergeant Pilot Jack Brundle RNZAF whose Stirling Bomber crashed nearby in February 1943. The Park is occasionally open to the public.

Southampton, The Alliance Hotel, Oxford Street, was requisitioned to provide temporary accommodation for Canadian Firefighters stationed in the city. The hotel is now known as the White Star serving as a pub with accommodation.

Basingstoke, The Wheatsheaf Hotel, Winton Square. A blue plaque erected here is dedicated to Major John Howard. Along with other officers from the 1st Airlanding Brigade, Major Howard played a vital role in the D-Day campaign. In January 1942, he and fellow officers arrived in Basingstoke and made their Mess at The Wheatsheaf. Major Howard was instrumental in leading the capture of the key Pegasus Bridge and in so doing, he prevented German forces from flanking the Allied forces landing at Sword Beach on D-Day. Kempshott Park, on the outskirts of the town, was a centre for the development of Flame Throwers.

Within the Southern Command area, which embraced Hampshire, over 800 shell proof pillboxes were built, and nearly 50 Anti-Tank defences installed. There were 80 naval guns, and 250 bullet proof pillboxes. At the time, some 60,000 troops and civilians were engaged on defensive construction work, building pill boxes, Anti-Tank traps, sea defences, laying land mines and placing demolition charges on bridges and on the airfields across the county.

*At the outbreak of the war, the Government decided that it would be necessary to build cold stores to supplement the capacity that the trade had. Lord Woolton arrived at an agreement in November 1940, with the cold storage industry about the future of any cold store that should be built. Any stores that were built for the Government and on Government account, should be on the basis that they should be retained on a care-and-maintenance basis as a permanent reserve, or they should be dismantled and the sites sold or disposed of, or they should be offered to the industry at a price determined by an independent valuation. During the war the

Government built cold storage capacity amounting to about 15 million cubic feet, which was about one-third of the total cold storage capacity of the country. The buildings programme cost was £7 million.

Military Museums

Army Flying Museum
MiddleWallop, Stockbridge, near Andover.
https://armyflying.com

Solent Sky Museum
Southampton.

Portsmouth Historic Dockyard & related Museums
Portsmouth.

Aldershot Military Museum
Queens Avenue, Aldershot.

Milestones Living History Museum
Basingstoke.

Royal Navy Submarine Museum
Gosport.

Museum of Military Medicine
Aldershot.

Hurst Castle
Keyhaven, via Milford on Sea.

The Gurkha Museum
Winchester.
Royal Army Physical Training Corps Museum
Aldershot.

Royal Victoria Chapel
Netley, Southampton.

Peninsula Barracks and Winchester Military Museums
Winchester.

Links to many of the museums can be found on the visit Hampshire site:
https://www.visit-hampshire.co.uk/militaryattractions

Field Marshal Alan Francis Brooke, 1st Viscount Alanbrooke, KG, GCB, OM, GCVO, DSO & Bar
The Field Marshall lived in Hartley Witney, Hampshire. He is laid to rest at St Johns Church in the village.

Field Marshal Bernard Law Montgomery, 1st Viscount Montgomery of Alamein, KG, GCB, DSO, PC, DL
'Monty' lived near Alton, Hampshire. He is laid to rest in Binstead, at Holy Cross Church.

Admiral of the Fleet Louis Francis Albert Victor Nicholas Mountbatten, 1st Earl Mountbatten of Burma lived in Romsey, Hampshire. He is laid to rest in Romsey Abbey.

A reminder please to check the status of the locations and sites as mentioned above, before travelling or exploring. Some sites are accessible, other sites can be seen from the public highway or public footpath. However, sites where known to be in private ownership are identified either in text, or with the symbol (P) and access must be regarded as prohibited.

All information is considered correct at the time of publication. Every reasonable effort has been made to ensure accuracy. Should there be notified corrections, they will be acknowledged in any future edition. You are welcome to write with relevant enquiries about the contents, the use of material and for any other information. Please contact www.sabrestorm.com

Stanbridge Earls near Romsey was a rest home for US flying crews. It is now a private residential area (Stanbridge Earls)

One of the surviving pillboxes at Worthy Down Winchester (Marc Heighway)

Administering the Penny a Week Fund at Bramshill House Hartley Wintney
(John Morgans)

A section of Paulsgrove Radio Station, Portsmouth (Marc Heighway)

The railway now known as the Mid Hants Heritage Railway used to carry troops to Southampton as well as ballast to New Forest Airfields (AC)

Cricket matches were one of the Holiday at Home activities organised by local groups and organisations (Argos)

The plaque at the base of a memorial tree in Rotherfield Park, near Alton (AC)

Broad Street, Alresford, Hampshire (AC)

A Hampshire Home Guard Unit possibly Basingstoke, early war

D-Day Landing Craft at Gosport (HFRS)

King George 6 - 1940 Aldershot.
Queens Avenue during WW2 was the most famous and busiest parade ground in the country,
running as it did through the centre of the home of the British Army (AC)

Aldermaston airfield. Paratroopers boarding a C47 for another mission (AC)

On the former RAF Chilbolton airfield, near Stockbridge (AC)

On parade Aldershot 1939 (AC)

The front view of one of three pillboxes alongside the main London to Bournemouth railway near Odiham (AC)

Gillkicker Fort Gosport 2022 (Marc Heighway)

Northington, the remains of an oil pumping station. (AC)

A section of tunnel at Fort Southwick Portsdown, Portsmouth (Marc Heighway)

*At former RAF Lasham, near Alton remains of wartime
occupation can still be seen (AC)*

South Warnborough. Huts occupied by an NFS Overseas Contingent (HFRS)

This memorial at former RAF Lasham is one of many similar memorials that have been dedicated at WW2 airfields across the county (AC)

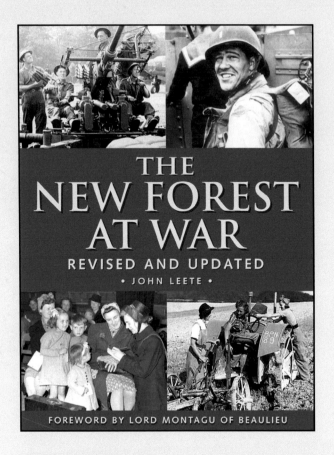

THE
NEW FOREST
AT WAR
REVISED AND UPDATED
• JOHN LEETE •

FOREWORD BY LORD MONTAGU OF BEAULIEU

Also by John Leete
The New Forest at War - Revised and Updated
ISBN: 9781781220030